Praise for *How Wealth*

MW00990419

"How Wealth Rules the W
ous social science academ
................y social change activists.
It convincingly exposes how property became and remains the single
most sacred and legally protected right in our culture and increasingly
globally, which has routinely blocked peoples' right to protect the health,
safety, and environment of their communities. Price challenges people
of conscience dedicated to human rights and protecting the planet
in our life-threatening times to rethink their goals and reassess their
strategies directed toward authentic life-affirming systemic change."

—Greg Coleridge, Outreach Director, Move to Amend

"Powerfully and unflinchingly, Ben Price is telling the truth: the truth
about the founding of our nation, our legal system, the mess we're
in—and what we can do to change it. Well said, every word, and all
true. It is staggering to realize that the architecture of this country
was (and still is) designed to deliver injustice and inequality in perpetuity unless we work for real change. I appreciated the in-depth
historical and contemporary look at this issue. It's a bit overwhelming
to realize the depth of revolution required if we are ever to see real
democracy here in the United States, but Price guides us through the
challenges to the opportunities with depth, intensity, and dedication
to getting to the vision that so many of us hold for people-powered
democracy. An important read."

—Rivera Sun, author of *The Dandelion Insurrection*

"Ben Price's important new book, *How Wealth Rules the World*, is
a revelatory page-turner, an urgent and timely guide to both explain
the subversion of democracy by the rich and to provide a way out of
the meat grinder that is shredding and destroying families, communities, countries, and our planet's very biosphere, its ability to sustain
nature and civilizations.

"The counterrevolution of business and property over we the
people, our rights and communities, has grown ever stronger for
hundreds of years as American courts and politicians serving the
elite have subverted our branches of government. Read *How Wealth
Rules the World*, share it, discuss it, and organize around it as if your
family's and friends' lives depended on it—because they do."

**—John Stauber, author of bestsellers including *Toxic Sludge Is Good for
You*; *Trust Us, We're Experts*; and *Weapons of Mass Deception***

"Unlike good ice cream, the truth can be hard to swallow. But you won't get a brain-freeze from reading this book. Dig into *Ben Price's How Wealth Rules the World*. I promise; it'll be good for you. He's scooped the political historians by serving up unexpected revelations chock-full of common sense."

—Jerry Greenfield, cofounder of Ben & Jerry's

"*How Wealth Rules the World* is an immensely important revelatory work that lifts the blanket off this still insufficiently discussed but absolutely most important issue. Ben Price offers a step-by-step explanation of the extent to which the wealthiest 1 percent of the population have managed to usurp control and undermine the once democratic processes in the United States, distorting them to serve only the goals of the richest people on the planet. This information is mandatory for anyone interested in pursuing positive change, and Ben Price has done a magnificent, step-by-step presentation of the roots and details of the problem. Right now, this is probably the most important subject we all need to address. Thank you to Ben Price for moving the details forward."

—Jerry Mander, author of *Four Arguments for the Elimination of Television* and *The Capitalism Papers*

HOW WEALTH RULES THE WORLD

SAVING OUR COMMUNITIES AND FREEDOMS FROM THE DICTATORSHIP OF PROPERTY

BEN G. PRICE

FOREWORD BY DAVID C. KORTEN, AUTHOR OF *WHEN CORPORATIONS RULE THE WORLD*

BK®

Berrett-Koehler Publishers, Inc.

Berrett-Koehler Publishers, Inc.
1333 Broadway, Suite 1000
Oakland, CA 94612-1921
Tel: (510) 817-2277   Fax: (510) 817-2278   www.bkconnection.com

Ordering Information

Quantity sales. Special discounts are available on quantity purchases by corporations, associations, and others. For details, contact the "Special Sales Department" at the Berrett-Koehler address above.

Individual sales. Berrett-Koehler publications are available through most bookstores. They can also be ordered directly from Berrett-Koehler: Tel: (800) 929-2929; Fax: (802) 864-7626; www.bkconnection.com

Orders for college textbook/course adoption use. Please contact Berrett-Koehler: Tel: (800) 929-2929; Fax: (802) 864-7626.

Distributed to the U.S. trade and internationally by Penguin Random House Publisher Services.

Berrett-Koehler and the BK logo are registered trademarks of Berrett-Koehler Publishers, Inc.

Printed in the United States of America

Berrett-Koehler books are printed on long-lasting acid-free paper. When it is available, we choose paper that has been manufactured by environmentally responsible processes. These may include using trees grown in sustainable forests, incorporating recycled paper, minimizing chlorine in bleaching, or recycling the energy produced at the paper mill.

Library of Congress Cataloging-in-Publication Data

Names: Price, Ben G., author.
Title: How wealth rules the world : saving our communities and freedoms from the dictatorship of property / Ben G. Price.
Description: 1st Edition. | Oakland, CA : Berrett-Koehler Publishers, 2019.
Identifiers: LCCN 2018050755 | ISBN 9781523097630 (paperback)
Subjects: LCSH: Wealth—United States. | Right of property—United States. | United States. Constitution. | BISAC: POLITICAL SCIENCE / Political Process / Political Advocacy. | POLITICAL SCIENCE / Economic Conditions. | LAW / Housing & Urban Development.
Classification: LCC HC110.W4 P74 2019 | DDC 339.20973—dc23
LC record available at https://lccn.loc.gov/2018050755

FIRST EDITION

25   24   23   22   21   20   19   10 9 8 7 6 5 4 3 2 1

Production manager: Susan Geraghty
Cover design: Wes Youssi, M.80 Design
Interior design and composition: Westchester Publishing Services
Copyeditor: Michele D. Jones
Proofreader: Sophia Ho
Indexer: Sylvia Coates
Author photo: Kara Scott

I dedicate this book to the people of every community struggling for control of their own destinies, and to my colleagues at the Community Environmental Legal Defense Fund, for their selfless commitment to making the future better and their devotion to correcting the errors of the past.

Contents

Foreword   vii
David C. Korten

Preface   xiii

Introduction   One Right to Rule Them All:
The Dark Side of Property   1

1. Property Is Not an Unalienable Right   23

2. The Ongoing Counterrevolution   47

3. Of Laws and Men   64

4. The Emancipation of Property from Democracy   89

5. The Municipal Colonies of America   103

6. The New Three-Fifths Clause   121

7. The Pretense of Representation   138

8. Creditors and Cannibals   149

9. Property's International Empire   163

Conclusion   Community Rights Challenge the
Dictatorship of Property   175

Notes   193
Acknowledgments   203
Index   207
About the Author   243

Contents

Foreword

We the people of the United States are not the middle-class democracy of, by, and for the people many of us grew up believing our nation to be. Our current awakening to this truth is a first step toward achieving our aspiration of real democracy and a society that truly works for all.

To take the next step, we must understand why achieving the aspiration has so long eluded us. This makes Ben Price's book, *How Wealth Rules the World*, a distinctive and essential read for our time.

I was among those who grew up believing that the United States modeled the middle-class democracy to which most of the world's people aspire. With that belief as my guide, I devoted some thirty years of my early professional life to sharing the supposed lessons of US success with the world's less fortunate. This included twenty-one years living and working as a development professional in Ethiopia, Central America, the Philippines, and Indonesia.

Over these years, I began to see results very different from what I had gone abroad to serve. I observed "development" forcing people off the lands and waters from which they met their daily needs. A tiny number of people were lifted to new levels of opulence and a few to new levels of material comfort. Most, however, were reduced to a daily struggle to survive even more brutal than the hardships they might previously have endured.

The real shock came when I realized that many in so-called advanced countries, including the United States, were experiencing a similar downward spiral. Eventually, I returned home to share what I had learned while abroad about the truth behind America's global mission. I documented that story in my book *When Corporations Rule the World.*

In *How Wealth Rules the World,* Price adds another layer of analysis to reveal a yet deeper truth and its roots in US history. He reveals how the inspiring and visionary words of the US Declaration of Independence mask the reality that the United States was born of the European conquest of the Western hemisphere, the theft of lands from the hemisphere's indigenous people, and the conversion of those lands into prosperous plantations by indentured servants fleeing extreme poverty in Europe and by slaves brutally abducted from Africa.

The rules of the new nation were written by members of a landed aristocracy resting on a foundation of stolen lands worked by their enslaved and indentured servants. Exactly whose rights and freedoms might we have expected these founder's preferred rules to guarantee?

It would come as no surprise that, as Price reminds us, the original US Constitution limited political power to white male property owners *and* that the first human rights victory of the citizens of the new nation came when white males without property won the right to vote. Nonwhite males followed only much later. Women, of course, came later still.

So, do we in the United States finally have democracy? Hardly. We are no longer ruled by a landed gentry, but rule remains in the hands of a propertied aristocracy. It isn't just some innocent fluke of history.

As Price elaborates, the legal code of the rights of property was inserted into the Constitution written by and for the owners of stolen property and the enslaved who worked it. It is not much of a stretch to suggest that the original Constitution was written to enshrine a US dictatorship of the propertied class.

I'm especially intrigued by the distinction Price makes between *personal* property that an individual has earned through his or her labor and *privileged* property that secures the rights of a propertied elite.

I often note that I believe private property is such a good thing that everyone should have some. By this I mean that all people should have a secure right to the property on which they depend for their basic livelihood. The land, tools, skills, and/or business from which the person makes a living for herself and her family. The place of lodging he calls home. These are the things in which every person should have an ownership stake as an individual or as a family or cooperative member.

Privileged property, as Price describes it, is property used by one person to extract unearned profits and/or to enjoy luxuries far beyond his personal need by controlling and limiting or prohibiting access by others to a means of living. It is a very important distinction between the right to make a living and the right to make a killing.

As Price describes, using a clever legal sleight of hand, the founders who drafted the Constitution made property into a rights-bearing canteen to be drunk from only by the holders of privileged property. They thereby assured that a propertied aristocracy of men like themselves would hold the powers of self-governance securely in their own exclusive hands.

As subsequent human rights victories led to constitutional amendments that weakened the rights of the propertied, a judiciary schooled in rights-of-property legal doctrine regularly stepped in to assume for itself the Constitutional power to issue decisions that restored and strengthened the founders' "original intention."

Consequently, the real power in our system resides not with We the People, or even with the institutions that make the rules. It resides with a court system that has taken unto itself the power to *interpret* the rules. This all comes together to secure the power of the US Supreme Court—as ultimate representative of the interests of the owners of privileged property—to be the ultimate decider among the three branches of the US government.

I have long suspected that the founders might well have anticipated that a Supreme Court staffed by graduates of elite law schools—in their day exclusively white males born of wealthy families—would be the ultimate arbiter of the rules. I have also long wondered about the twisted legal logic of the Supreme Court justices who granted the rights of personhood to corporations owned by private shareholders. Isn't an owned person a slave?

The system of rule by property in the name of democracy that the US founders put in place is one of history's greatest and most successful deceptions. Libertarian think tanks, neoliberal economists, and lawyers in service to the propertied class have more recently taken the deception global through the World Trade Organization and international trade and investment agreements.

I am struck by the truth of Price's extraordinary and perceptive observation that the US Constitution, which defined economic relations between thirteen formerly independent colonies with its clauses on contracts and interstate commerce, was effectively the first North American trade agreement securing the interests of big business and wealth concentration.

The division between the super-rich and everyone else continues to grow on a now global scale to create the greatest wealth gap in human history. As of 2018, the six richest people in the world owned more wealth than the poorest half of humanity. The combined wealth of the three richest US citizens exceeded that of the poorest half of the US population.[1]

If democracy was the founders' intention, they failed terribly. If it was to secure elite privilege and an ever-growing gap between rich and poor, they succeeded beyond anything they could possibly have imagined.

What the US founders may have intended, however, is currently irrelevant. We the People—*all people*—have the right and the imperative to create the democracy of the people, by the people, and for the people that we have never had. *How Wealth Rules the World* unlocks the code that stripped us of our rights and that we must now strip from the laws and legal institutions by which we govern ourselves.

David C. Korten, author, *When Corporations Rule the World* and *Change the Story, Change the Future: A Living Economy for a Living Earth*

Preface

A concerted assault on local democracy is under way. In towns, counties, villages, and cities across the United States and around the globe, municipalities are forbidden the authority to secure and protect residents' rights through local law.

Every day, people are faced with assaults against their rights on the job. They are left helpless to preserve their local economies against giant retail chains, subsidies paid with their tax dollars to attract community-busting monopolies, exemptions from local laws and taxes for industries that bring poverty-level wages and toxic by-products for local disposal. They are stripped of self-governing tools to defend the air they breathe against the installation of refineries and fossil fuel pipelines. They are scoffed at for wanting to protect their families and neighbors against police violence. They can't protect the land they get their food from and the air their children breathe against aerial pesticide spraying by agribusiness juggernauts. And it's illegal for them to safeguard the water their children drink against polluting manufacturers and extractors when state law forbids ("preempts") protective local laws.

The plan of this book is to unmask the artifice of democratic representation that American law—and the laws of many erstwhile democratic nations—mocks in practice. It will expose the way the legal system has been engineered to guarantee that wealth and empire prevail over people and their common birthright. It has been written for anyone who wonders "what went wrong" in a nation thought to have pioneered a system of democratic representation with rules that apply equally to everyone.

Community activists, labor leaders, working people, environmentalists, progressives tired of losing, and conservatives tired of believing in but not seeing reverence for foundational ideals will be interested in knowing how things got so screwed up.

Readers seeking a deeper understanding of why so many social and political challenges seem insurmountable and those who wonder why the legal system, economic policies, and international trade agreements seem to serve some purpose other than the public welfare will find in this book a new framework for productive thought.

Those involved with Move to Amend, Public Citizen, and similar organizations focused on ending the legal advantages with which courts have empowered corporations will find here an expanded and more nuanced view of the problem. Others whose critique of capitalism demands more than superficial reform will be interested to learn the hidden ways the wealthy are favored by a system of law that protects capitalism from democracy and sacrifices human and civil rights to ensure its success.

The information that people under siege need is not warm and fuzzy. It's stark and real. It may at times seem depressing, disempowering, and, frankly, not filled with hope. I can only say that, although these are common reactions to being exposed to our dire situation, that's not where the story ends. Extraordinary people have taken up the struggle for true freedom. They have begun to take seriously their unalienable right to protect themselves, their communities, and their natural environment against toxic uses of private wealth. *Unalienable,* as used in these pages, means intrinsic; impossible to be separated from; not able to be forfeited, sold, traded, or even voluntarily surrendered.

Understanding the truth of our predicament always seemed more important to my colleagues and me than being sensitive to the desire to find easy answers and quick fixes. Our impatience with Band-Aid solutions to systemic oppression is driven not by callousness but by urgency. Our critique of traditional progressive organizing is a judgment not of character but of strategy.

The underlying framework for what's revealed in these pages is partially outlined in the curriculum we've developed and continue to revise in what we call Democracy School. It's an intensive seminar that the Community Environmental Legal Defense Fund (CELDF) has presented to many hundreds of communities around the country since 2003. I'm a Democracy School lecturer, a contributor to the curriculum, and the current national organizing director for CELDF.

My community organizing work over the past fifteen years has been as important in developing the ideas presented here as the legal and historic research. At CELDF we've gone beyond theory and history. I was CELDF's first community rights organizer. Fifteen years later, with a team of organizers in multiple states, we've helped hundreds of communities draft local laws that challenge legal privileges for wealth that violate the rights of people and the natural world.

Along the way we learned how the system is *fixed*. It works exactly as intended. It prevents democracy from inconveniencing the rich. When I use the term *democracy*, I mean that the people affected by governing decisions are the ones who make and enforce the law, directly or through representatives bound to the will of the governed and limited only by a strict respect for the unalienable rights of all beings.

Rich people hiding behind the legal immunities afforded by incorporation appeal to domestic courts and international trade tribunals to protect their interests against democracy. Laws, administrative agencies, and a plethora of ineffective regulations are programmed to favor and maximize advantages for the privileged. Around the world, legal traditions rooted deep in the hierarchical imperialism of a globe-spanning empire yield predictably undemocratic results. In nations that have emulated the US Constitution and system of law, and in others that once were colonies of the British Empire, as was the United States, the dictatorship of property is mistaken as the indispensable foundation of civilization.

The story of how property gained through conquest and confiscation is legally immunized from democratic governance has been kept quiet for far too long. Today's beneficiaries of the colonial tradition of genocide, slavery, and ecocide have a responsibility to educate themselves to the facts and abandon the heroic legends that mask the truth.

Victims of empire around the world don't need to learn the visceral lessons that privileged white descendants of imperial colonizers need to learn. But before the progeny of settlers can understand the misery and injustice brought on by their forebearers, a lot of false history needs to be unlearned, including how, after American independence, counterrevolutionary schemers erected a system of government that perpetuates the violently won gains of wealthy white men.

This is your invitation to know what those who game the system know and to pick up where the American revolutionaries left off. Come join the community rights movement. It's time we liberate ourselves from our delusions and from the dictatorial power that law conveys to a propertied aristocracy.

One Right to Rule Them All

THE DARK SIDE OF PROPERTY

When plunder becomes a way of life for a group of men living together in society, they create for themselves in the course of time, a legal system that authorizes it and a moral code that glorifies it.

—Frederic Bastiat

Owning Up to the Real Problem: Wealth Obliterates Self-Government

Let's get it out in the open: The United States of America and nations that emulate its governing principles are governed by a dictatorship of property. Is it plutocracy? Sure, but it goes deeper than that.

The US Constitution, as it was written and later interpreted by the Supreme Court, hijacked democratic rights that American revolutionaries thought they had won. The Federalists developed a whole system of law that serves the interests of wealth. Elements of that system include the following:

❖ State constitutions untethered from their revolutionary moorings

❖ International trade agreements that supersede local, state, and federal laws

❖ Regulations administered by an unrepresentative bureaucracy

❖ Political parties that gerrymander legislative districts, so that they can choose their voters rather than allowing voters to choose representatives

❖ Corporate property that the Supreme Court has declared to be "persons" with Bill of Rights protections

❖ Federal and state statutes that privatize public governance and prohibit democratic limits on the uses of private fortunes

❖ Local governments declared to be property of the state and made unavailable to communities for municipal lawmaking

We live deep within an undemocratic matrix of law that masquerades as a democratic republic while it legalizes an aristocracy of wealth. The US Constitution was written by men who came from a uniformly privileged class. Charles Beard argued this point in his book *An Economic Interpretation of the Constitution of the United States.*[1] Beard analyzed the economic interests of those who met in secret to overturn the Articles of Confederation (the first constitution of the United States) and concluded that the Federalists were motivated by economic self-interest to establish a form of government that would protect their wealth against "an excess of democracy," as Alexander Hamilton put it.[2]

The Federalists who replaced the Articles with the US Constitution were not fully aligned with the liberating agenda of commoners who risked their lives to throw off the hierarchical chains of the British Empire. They were wealthy men educated in British law with opinions that harmonized with aristocratic sentiments.

The authors of the US Constitution are often called the "founding fathers." Popular history lumps the Federalist counterrevolutionaries in with the likes of Thomas Paine, who with his firebrand writings against monarchy, nobility, and special privileges for the few inspired the people to demand independence. Popular culture counts the Federalists as American Revolutionaries no less fervent for liberty than the men whose ideas of leveling the social class system inspired American farmers and day laborers to pick up their muskets and take on the Redcoats.

This conflation of the Federalist counterrevolutionaries with those whose "Spirit of '76" is reflected in the Declaration of Independence and absent from the US Constitution is a troubling reminder that popular history too often preserves false memories.

What's the evidence that the Federalists intended a constitution that weaponizes law to protect the accumulation of property and raise wealth above and out of reach of public governance? To begin with, their own words were recorded in Philadelphia in 1787 by James Madison and Robert Yates. Damningly, that record was held secret until every delegate to the clandestine conclave had died and the constitution they wrote had been the law of the land for two generations. We have that evidence, and it tells the tale I'll share in chapter 2.

We also have the product of their cleverness to consider. The Federalists established a quasi-monarchical judiciary. Politically appointed judges wield the power to veto any legislation that departs from the Federalists' original intent: to protect wealth accumulation from democratic oversight. We have the arguments of the Anti-Federalists who called out the would-be American aristocrats for betraying the Revolution.

If not for them, we would not have the first ten amendments to the Federalists' document, the Bill of Rights, which many identify as the soul of the US Constitution.

More immediate evidence that the original intent of the US Constitution was to immunize possession of unearned property from public regulation can be found in the antisocial way the document is interpreted by the courts and how it operates on society today.

The Dictatorship of Property

Here's my argument in a nutshell.

We are faced with social, political, and environmental problems that resist resolution because law empowers a wealthy minority to govern based on priorities often at odds with the general welfare. The Constitution—and its interpretation by the courts—amounts to an arsenal of weaponized law able to deliver special privileges to a propertied class. Certain legal mechanisms let those seeking to profit at the public expense block policies that compete with their interests.

These legal doctrines operate by a two-step process. First, they remove democratic rights from the public sphere and deposit them in concentrated accumulations of property. The oddity of attaching legal rights to property itself rather than to people roared into public consciousness with the Supreme Court's 2010 *Citizens United* ruling that affirmed corporate property's "personhood" and free speech rights. Although the ruling shocked the conscience of average Americans, it was not the first time the Court had vested civil rights within inert property. Nor were corporations the first type of property to be given legal rights.

The second step is for property imbued with rights to deliver those rights as an extra layer of legal privilege to the property owner.

When civil and human rights are deposited in property, that property is placed beyond the authority of the people to govern how it is used by its owner. This nullifies the majority's ability to decide directly or through elected representatives what the public policy will be.

As a result, we aren't allowed to resolve issues of immediate concern to every community. Even when we understand what needs to be done, we are often blocked. Privileges secured by law for an opulent minority outweigh our right to self-govern. We're left institutionally powerless when the interests of the rich conflict with settling issues like these through community lawmaking:

❖ Homelessness

❖ Police accountability

❖ Sanctuary cities, immigrants' rights

❖ Workers' rights on the job

❖ Minimum/living wage

❖ Fracking

❖ Retail chains

❖ Water privatization

❖ Genetically modified plants and animals (GMOs)

❖ Gun regulation

❖ School privatization

❖ Private vote tallying

❖ Corporatization of food production

❖ Prisoners' rights

- ❖ Prison privatization

- ❖ Unsustainable energy policies

- ❖ "Private" surveillance and data mining

- ❖ Factory farms

- ❖ Strip mining

- ❖ Predatory lending

- ❖ Pipelines

- ❖ Urban sewage sludge

- ❖ Toxic trespass (private poisoning of the public)

Our social and governing problems are rooted in the legal fiction of property. I say "legal fiction" because without law, property does not exist, as we'll discuss thoroughly in chapter 1. For now, it's important to realize that not all property conveys the same kind of governing clout to its owner. To make this clearer, I'll draw a distinction between *personal property* and *privileged property.*

Personal property, as used in these pages, is derived from one's own labor. Ownership of it is understandably a cherished right. Our homes and vehicles, our wages and savings (not "returns" on savings derived from interest)—these justly belong to each of us, meaning we have an exclusive right to them. The right to own the fruit of one's personal effort is unalienable. Again, *unalienable* means intrinsic; impossible to be separated from; not able to be forfeited, sold, traded, or even voluntarily surrendered.

The right to one's personal property is part of the right of self-preservation and includes the right of material security within the social context and within the natural ecosystem. Personal property is a limited category, confined to what an individual can produce solely from personal effort. It may be just enough to subsist; it may be a significant treasure. But it is never accumulated at the expense of someone else's rights.

Privileged property is the kind of property to which the Federalists, and later their quasi-monarchical Supreme Court, attached legal privileges—the kind of property that is *not* earned by personal effort. Either it is the spoils of conquest, the booty of pillaging, or the result of the enclosure (privatization) of "the commons," or it is ownership of amassed property through inheritance, purchase, garnishment, or confiscation.

Privileged property involves monopoly control, including the deprivation of the rights of others. It is accumulated and maintained by many mechanisms, including rationing of necessities and extortion of labor in exchange for them. Ownership of privileged property is regularly used to justify extractive activities that destroy the ability of human communities and ecosystems to sustain a healthy existence.

I am not claiming that privileged property is always used in antisocial ways. Large fortunes amassed by robber barons, real estate moguls, televangelists, and dictators are enjoyed through inheritance by their children, who sometimes apply a part of the hoard to philanthropic causes. Even when it is used for seemingly noble purposes, however, privileged property is still the result of anti-social behavior. Pierre-Joseph Proudhon (author of *What Is Property?* 1840), said of it, "Property is theft."

The legal doctrines that institutionalized special privilege for the wealthy include the following:

- ❖ Federal preemption of state and local commercial law-making

- ❖ Privatization of public law

- ❖ Commoditization of unalienable rights by way of contract (e.g., mandatory waiver of rights to enter into routine business contracts; mandatory arbitration and juryless settlements)

- ❖ Corporate "rights"

- ❖ The denial of legal "standing" to appear in court without a property claim

- ❖ Subordination of local governments through state preemption (prohibitions on local law making)

- ❖ Legal biases in favor of the property rights of creditors and against the human rights of debtors

- ❖ The dictatorship of precedent over justice

- ❖ And many other devices

The rich handily override the rights of individuals and the will of community majorities. When our solutions to local harms involve restricting the use of accumulated wealth, the wealthy rely on rights vested in property to stop us. And the law is on their side.

At the time of this writing, I've been working with citizens in Denver, Colorado, to place a "right to survive" amendment to the city charter on the ballot. Its intent is to secure the rights of people who are homeless against constant harassment and move-on orders by local law enforcement. Those orders serve the interests of the business community, but they violate the fundamental rights of propertyless persons, who lack the legal protections afforded to wealth.

People deal with homelessness and all the other local challenges one at a time, as though they are unrelated. Activists organize locally to stop a gas pipeline, address police violence, object to aerial pesticide spraying, advocate for prisoners' rights, demand a living wage, prohibit the injection of toxic fracking waste into the same ground from which they draw their drinking water. They believe that there are regulations and protective laws they can invoke to their advantage. But most people who confront these issues run into the same wall. Just when they think they can't lose because their cause is just and they've gathered all the damning evidence they need to prove their case, it all gets wiped away.

People are frustrated by unreceptive courts and left baffled by negative outcomes. They feel blindsided. They begin to blame themselves for missing small details, for not organizing better, or for not figuring out how to navigate a complex system of law. When people ask regulatory agencies and elected representatives for protection, they are routinely told there's nothing to be done. Their local officials shrug and say that they wish they could help, but their hands are tied.

What these activists generally don't realize is that the outcome was in every case predetermined. It's not their fault. Rather than ensuring equal rights for all of us, our property-based legal system conveys privileged access to power to those who possess wealth, while denying it to everyone else. Issues that undeniably affect whole communities are decided by the courts primarily based on property claims. Contracts and corporate law are said to relate to matters of a private interests and are of no interest to the public. Using this reasoning, they are said to fall within the realm of *private law*. As such, they are removed from the public sphere and immunized from public governance.

This privatization of law dealing with contracts and corporations treats the whole realm of economic behavior as if it had no impact on society at-large. It follows a logic that has as its premise the notion that individuals with wealth should decide all matters defined as "commerce" free from public interference. This explains our inability to make democratic decisions about many issues. Once removed from the purview of *public law,* the priorities of wealth are deemed off-limits to public governance. Public law is, of course, the kind we are most familiar with. It sets policies and places sanctions on anti-social behavior. It deals with issues of general concern to the community at-large. Our right to make public policies on issues in which wealth has an interest has been privatized. As a result, we are institutionally powerless.

Here's How We Know Whom Government Serves

By the mid-twentieth century, state governments were routinely being recruited by the corporate class to further curtail local self-governing rights. By the second decade of the twenty-first century, the practice of knee-jerk preemption (overruling) of the power of municipalities to govern corporate behavior moved with precision.

Municipalities are the institutions most commonly available to citizens for exercising the right of self-government. State preemption of local lawmaking frequently amounts to usurpation of public governance to benefit private interests. The courts regularly deny that preemption deprives people of their democratic rights, but forbidding municipalities to enact laws that protect the rights of people accomplishes just that. Underlying these rulings, the courts presume that the people never had authority to employ the states' property for their own purposes.

Dillon's Rule, which we'll hear more about in chapter 5, is the legal theory that community governments are utterly subordinate to the state. It is asserted day in and day out, not by states intervening directly into municipal affairs, but by the managers and directors of business corporations suing local governments to overturn laws that interfere with their agendas. When they sue, they ask the court to rule that the municipality has acted outside of its valid authority in adopting a law prohibiting a corporate project. Predictably, industry front groups and lobbyists have already succeeded in having the state institute preemptive laws that the corporate lawyers then invoke to their advantage.

Preemption is a term that applies in situations where federal law blocks state law, and where state law trumps local law. The reason for a higher level of government to block lawmaking at a lower level is that some interested party has a claim that is prior and superior to the interests of everyone else. When fundamental rights are being protected by local law, the higher law can set minimal protections and forbid state or local legislation that weakens those protections. This is called *floor preemption,* and it is a legitimate protection of civil rights. When floor preemption is exercised, unalienable rights and other keystone values are held superior to other considerations.

Ceiling preemption works in the opposite direction. When rights in property are at risk of being diminished by a local law, the state sets *maximum* protections and forbids the municipality to legislate in a way that would exceed state regulations and protect the community more than the state allows. Ceiling preemption protects the interests of wealth against the interests of justice and is therefore illegitimate.

Ceiling preemption means that the state regulations will be minimal. It also means that wealthy speculators, investors, corporations, and developers can rest assured that municipal governments will not interfere with their primary goal of extracting profit from the community.

More significantly, ceiling preemptions are enforced through litigation by publicly chartered and licensed "private" corporations. The rights with which law imbues property empower corporate management to use the courts to strike down municipal laws that fail to show deference to the propertied class. Even though a preemptive law is adopted by the state, it is the wealthy people using the corporation and the extra rights attached to it who bring legal actions to usurp local governing rights and enlist the courts to enforce the preemption. Because it is enforced privately rather than by the government that enacts it, the supposedly *public law* of ceiling preemption amounts to the privatization of public governing authority.

Liberating Communities to Protect Themselves: Making Government Serve the Governed

It took only a couple of years for my colleagues and me to figure out that corporations and their court-bestowed rights aren't the root of the problem. They're a symptom. Our basic premise was that unalienable rights belong to the living and that they are higher law when it comes to a contest of legitimacy with rights stored in amassed property and conveyed to its owners. We started applying that basic premise to challenge each of the Federalists' property-as-sovereignty legal doctrines.

Then we took the next step. People resisting state-permitted dumping of toxic waste in their communities thought there was no way around laws preempting local bans. But if we take seriously the primacy of unalienable rights, and that "democracy" means that the people affected by governing decisions are the ones to make those decisions, then state and federal preemptions forbidding local rights-protecting laws are illegitimate by logical extension.

That's why we began including in the local laws we drafted language that specifically nullifies permits that pretend to legalize what the community banned to protect its health, safety, and environment. In Youngstown, Ohio, for example, residents have tried to amend their city charter—a local constitution—seven times, as of this writing. They've attempted to enact a Community Bill of Rights that would ban fracking and related infrastructure. They've been beaten back each time by a large influx of corporate money spent on scare tactics and misinformation.

When the community came within less than a percentage point of winning in 2016, a whole new opposition strategy unfolded the next time they tried. The state teamed up with the propertied class to keep the people's proposed law off the ballot and prevent the voters from deciding. Industry honchos were tired of spending their money to thwart local democracy. They enlisted the state attorney general, the county boards of elections, and the courts to invent ever more tenuous legal reasons to block access to the ballot for the community's initiative. Even more galling, the people's own tax dollars were spent to defeat their efforts.

Thanks to CELDF Ohio organizer Tish O'Dell, the Protect Youngstown community group has not backed down, despite the withering opposition. They have a saying in Youngstown, after all these battles: "You don't lose until you quit." Every struggle for civil rights has come to the same conclusion.

One of the provisions included in their proposed amendment has been used over the years by dozens of communities in other states. It rejects the notion that the state can legalize activities that violate the rights of community members. The section says this: "No permit, license, privilege, or charter issued by any state, federal or international entity which would violate this Charter shall be deemed valid within the City of Youngstown."

Directly challenging long-standing legal doctrines is necessary because government has no legitimate authority to prohibit free people from protecting their rights with democratically enacted local laws. The right of the people to engage in self-government in their own communities is the essence of what community rights organizing is all about. Ceiling preemption, Dillon's Rule, and municipal subordination to state government are legal doctrines used not for the general welfare but by a propertied minority keen to upend the unalienable right of self-government when it encroaches on the privileges of wealth.

When the City Council of Pittsburgh, at the insistence of a mobilized community, defied the state's preemption and banned fracking in 2010, I discussed the implications of challenging doctrines like preemption with council members during the ordinance drafting process and in public testimony prior to the vote. With each new local law that we draft for our client communities, my colleagues and I include provisions that more completely address the violation of unalienable rights by the rights *of* property. Pittsburgh's ordinance challenged the state's authority to preempt rights-protecting prohibitions on fracking. It also denied corporate personhood and declared that "corporations in violation of the prohibition against natural gas extraction or seeking to engage in natural gas extraction shall not . . . be afforded the protections of the commerce or contract clauses within the United States

Constitution or corresponding sections of the Pennsylvania Constitution."

That's right. We took on the *commerce* and *contract clauses* of the US Constitution too, because they purport to enforce private privilege with public law and deprive fundamental rights in the process.

"We Wish We Could Help, but Our Hands Are Tied"

The lament of every municipal official confronted by a roomful of angry constituents could be summarized on a bumper sticker that says, "We wish we could help, but our hands are tied." It's the mantra that every one of us hears when we show up at a municipal meeting to ask local officials to do something to stop Project X. You know: the pipeline, the frack wells, the power lines and microwave towers, the landfill expansion, the big box store, the latest moneymaker that nobody wants.

The people we elect locally aren't universally apathetic about the needs of their communities. They generally do what they can with what they've got, which is less and less as states breach their responsibilities to citizens more and more to save money for other priorities, like tax cuts for the rich and subsidies for the biggest of businesses.

When they tell us they can't help us, our municipal officials are telling mostly the truth, although they always have a choice to buck the system and do what's right. The ones who will take that stand are the ones community rights organizers love to bump into. They are the salt of the earth, the ones who offer hope that the precedent-driven repetition of errors of the past can be corrected. They are the special ones who know that neither the state nor the federal government can legitimately forbid public servants from standing up for the rights of the neighbors who elected them. They understand that you can't protect wealth at the expense of everybody and everything else and pretend that's the way it should be.

Somebody Stole Our Revolution

By now many of us know that the US Supreme Court decided on its own, without direction from elected representatives of the people or precedent from judges of the past, that corporate property has constitutional rights. This is a prime example of what I mean when I say that law—including case law (the accumulated collection of court decisions)—lodges unalienable rights intended for people within property. The Supreme Court didn't invent the idea of stowing constitutional rights within inert property, although the choice of corporate property was a real innovation. They took their lead from the men who wrote the Constitution.

The Federalists got the ball rolling when they injected rights to extraordinary political representation within the privileged property of slaves. Until the Civil War, slaves counted as three-fifths of a person for purposes of proportional representation in the House of Representatives and delegates to the Electoral College. With the *three-fifths clause*, the Constitution injected political rights into human chattel and gave slave owners palpable political advantages over all American white males represented in nonslave states. The principle of one citizen–one vote was violated, even when only wealthy white males were granted suffrage. The patrician plantation culture of the South cut a deal with Northern proto-industrialists and avoided the most overt trappings of aristocracy in exchange for the political power of an aristocracy. Possession of privileged property (slaves) translated into superior power in the governance of the nation for otherwise outnumbered possessors of human chattel.

It must be said that neither inert corporate property nor enslaved people are able to enjoy the rights that the law deposits in them. They are mere vessels for conveying the rights *of* property to their owners, who capitalize on the extra political power thus conveyed. Corporations and slaves are examples of what I've been calling privileged property.

The original, unamended federal constitution included other methods of infusing privileged property with rights that convey superior political power to the best hoarders of capital. The power to govern, supposedly won by white male revolutionaries, was privatized and made unavailable even to the average unbanked white man on issues impinging on rights in wealth. This was accomplished by inclusion of such constitutional provisions as the commerce clause, the contract clause, and the fugitive labor clause. We're going to get to all that.

We'll examine each of these wealth-biased nuggets in later pages. They impose contractual obligations on each citizen, without the consent of each citizen, right there in the US Constitution. As we will see, the long-term effect has been to privatize decision-making on many issues that would otherwise reasonably be considered matters of public concern and democratic governance.

Over the past two hundred years, a succession of politically appointed Supreme Court judges has gone further than the Federalists dared by infusing all sorts of property with new governing powers that are transferable to the owners. Recent outrageous judicial decisions have caused an uptick in the number of people conscious of and alarmed by the ploy.

Citizens United v. Federal Elections Commission was the court case decided in 2010 in which the judges gave corporations a constitutional right to spend unlimited amounts of money to influence the outcome of elections. A sleeping public that hadn't noticed that American law already put the rich in the driver's seat was suddenly roused. Some thought that the worst thing about the decision was that corporations had been declared legal "persons." They hadn't been taught that the courts made that decision 124 years earlier. Few realized that the decision wasn't about corporations at all. It was about clearing the way for the wealthy to decide who will govern in the United States. A scattering of voices could be heard calling for a constitutional amendment to overturn the decision.

If they succeed, it won't be nearly enough.

Half-Fast Measures

The Supreme Court betrays every American with rulings like *Citizens United*, but that's only the tip of the iceberg. Since the beginning of the nineteenth century, the courts have found ways to include corporate property in the Constitution, although corporations are never mentioned there. Over time, devotion to the "founders" became a more powerful meme than fealty to the ideals of the Revolution. Our awareness of betrayal has been sublimated beneath the surface of American jingoism. This explains the general reluctance to demand systemic change.

The most drastic proposals from constitutional reformers go no further than calling for constitutional amendments to overturn the damage done by *Citizens United*. The short of it is this: It's a losing strategy. Because the legal mechanisms for conveying extra power and authority to the wealthy are deeply engrained in US law, those amendments would do little to free us from the dictatorship of property. There's no delicate way to say it: We have much bigger problems.

Today, wealth inequality is a hot topic, but the fact that rich people enjoy more leisure and luxury than the rest of us is not the problem. It's not just about corporations, either. Judges *regularly* attach legal privileges to property. Case law is a veritable La Brea Tar Pit filled with the preserved remnants of an extinct democracy, all covered in the black goo of legal doubletalk. Judges have solemnly doled out legal opinions, insisting that their job is to serve the law and not administer justice, all without making it clear that precedent and the laws they serve favor a propertied class of aristocrats.

We are at a moment in history when a movement is afoot to amplify and strengthen legal rights attached to wealth. Occasional "rogue" court decisions, such as *Citizens United*, are taken as the exception even though the US Supreme Court has never failed to preserve the law's protection of rights in property over the rights of people.

The court has regularly created new vessels to carry those privileges. Decisions like *Citizens United* are nothing new. They reinforce and expand the legal default settings that date back to 1789.

Making property into a rights-bearing canteen to be drunk from only by its owners guaranteed that we'd be ruled by an aristocracy of the propertied class and that we'd thirst for the deprived right of self-governance. The Federalists thought they knew better. We need to understand and believe they were wrong.

International House of Property: Wealth's Global Dominion

The tactic of storing legal rights and governing authority in property, initiated by the Federalists, has had profound impacts into the twenty-first century not only in the US but globally. Around the world, nations have histories steeped in colonialism, with all its brutality, enslavement, and exploitation. Although the US escaped its colonial chains earlier than many countries, its racist, misogynistic, homophobic culture preserved in its Constitution the oppressive inequities inherited from the British Empire. From the privatization of the commons (the "enclosures") to the treatment of women and Africans as chattel, Americans took inspiration for institutionalized injustice from the empire that succeeded in claiming as its own much of North America.

For good or ill, the US Constitution has been emulated by newly emancipated nation-states, so that many have adopted parts of it as their own. Others, once British colonies, have modeled their governments closer to that of their former imperial master. And fifty-three former colonies are aligned as members of the Commonwealth of Nations to this day. Over the past half century, neoliberalism and globalization have entrenched the acquisition of wealth and the centralization of control over trade, commerce, and finance as the core values of a planetary regime. International trade agreements are negotiated by those whose privileged property empowers them to act in the sphere of domestic and international governance as free agents. Stowing superior political rights in property may have a "Made in the USA" label on it, as a legal innovation, but by now it's as ubiquitous globally as jazz and rock 'n roll.

The niceties of republicanism, citizenship, representation, and even sovereignty have been courteously mooted. Turning the whole planet and its every aspect and inhabitant into commoditized property is no longer a patrician pipe dream. Totalitarian capitalism has been legalized. Protecting home, family, habitat, and the future from the dictatorship of property is illegal, pretty much no matter where you go.

Planetary Emancipation

There is a movement afoot that could undermine this dystopian reality. Internationally, a movement for the legally enforceable rights of nature is under way. It began humbly, in a little borough in Pennsylvania. It spread to Ecuador, Bolivia, New Zealand, and India. It has a life of its own, and that is why it is unstoppable.

How can recognizing the unalienable rights of nature challenge and defeat the global juggernaut of rights legally attached to property? The answer is in the question. When nature is no longer categorized in its every aspect as property, and when forests, mountaintops, aquifers, coal seams, ore deposits, genetic material, natural medicines, and every subset of the natural world are emancipated from the legal status of property, then the threat to our rights and our common inheritance posed by the hegemony of private ownership can be ended.

Humans are a part of the natural world. Although the grand philosophies that justified and inspired imperial conquests over other lands, people, and nature are based on the premise that some special humans exist apart from and above nature and have monopoly rights over it, that's simply not the case. We are one of many species on the tree of life, dependent for our breath, sustenance, and survival on all of it and exempt from none of its priorities.

Because so many still believe that the ideals of the Declaration of Independence are alive, if imperfectly, in the US Constitution and the government it spawned, it's not possible for many Americans to discover the truth right under their noses. But for people in nations more recently liberated from colonialism and exploitation, and in those nations still suffering under its power, the hypocrisy is more immediate. The unalienable rights bestowed on every one of us by "Nature . . . and Nature's God," as the Declaration has it, and the aspiration to establish government at the consent of the governed have been betrayed in America and around the world where those ideals gain no more than lip service. It is an unnatural situation.

An Invitation

The dictatorship of property has insinuated itself into our hometowns. It sits as a gatekeeper at all our town meetings in the seat of the municipal attorney who advises the erstwhile elected representatives of the people that they must ignore the will of the community and defer to the power and preemptions of their wealthy masters.

These are not idle claims. They are direct observations from the front lines of the community rights movement. If it all sounds too depressing and surreal in a country where the people are supposed to be in charge, take courage from the fact that there is hope. It's been here all along. But do take courage, because you'll need it. We're the ones we've been waiting for. It's time to wake up and act. Others have begun. You can join them.

Property Is Not an Unalienable Right

I doubt whether a single fact, known to the world, will carry as clear conviction to it . . . of the treasonable views of the federal party . . . who having nothing in them of the feelings or principles of '76 now look to a single and splendid government of an Aristocracy, founded on banking institutions and monied in corporations . . . This will be to them a next best blessing to the Monarchy of their first aim, and perhaps the surest stepping stone to it."

—Thomas Jefferson

Devise and Conquer: The Legal Foundations of Empire

In Lancaster County, Pennsylvania, residents have been trying to protect their community and environment from the Atlantic Sunrise pipeline since 2014. They organized under the banner "Lancaster Against Pipelines," and on October 17, 2017, twenty-three members of the group were arrested for blocking a backhoe from tearing into land owned by a group of nuns, the Adorers of the Blood of Christ.

The pipeline is intended to transport natural [sic] gas from frack wells scattered throughout the commonwealth to export terminals on the coast. The nuns' land, and an outdoor chapel they'd built on the part of their land seized through eminent domain, is in the path of the fossil fuel conduit. *Eminent domain* is government sanctioned appropriation of personal property for a supposed public use with compensation to the owner.

According to the *York Daily Record,* "The Adorers claim that the developer's seizure of the rights to the easement via eminent domain violated their religious freedom, since reverence for the land was among their deeply held spiritual beliefs."[1] The nuns had filed suit against the Federal Energy Regulatory Commission (FERC) for permitting the violation of their religious rights, but on this October day, as that lawsuit went unanswered by the court, part of the shrine was dismantled and trenches dug, after the peaceful protestors were removed.

In July 2018, the US Third Circuit Court of Appeals ruled against the nuns' claim that their religious rights were being violated. The community group Lancaster Against Pipelines put out a press release announcing the decision. They wrote, in part, "It's crystal clear from this ruling that the Natural Gas Act supersedes even our most fundamental Constitutional rights."

This confrontation reveals power dynamics that are important to understanding how our system of law arms wealth and disempowers those with less of it (or none). It's a contest between anonymous humans pushing for the Atlantic Sunrise pipeline, the residents opposing it, and the nuns whose land was taken lawfully and given to a corporation whose owners have plans to profit from the confiscated property.

The first dynamic to notice is that the law transferred control of the commandeered property to a private business corporation. The corporate directors had no plans to put the land to use for a public benefit. They intended to use it to generate profit by exporting gas to foreign markets. Eminent domain handed owners of corporate property the legal right to take possession of the nuns' property.

The second dynamic to notice is that, although rights vested in property under US law exceed the rights inherent in people and living systems, the law also distinguishes between wealth and mere possessions. The amount of property and whether it is personal property or privileged property makes all the difference.

The third dynamic to notice is that the law found greater value in the property rights of the owners of corporate property than the nuns' right of ownership to their land. The nuns' property and the preservation of their right to it do not serve the priorities of power and empire as much as advancing the corporation's interests.

Herein is revealed the difference between privileged property and nonprivileged personal property. If all property were the same in the eyes of the law, the nuns might have expected the courts to protect their right to it. Whom the law works for and whom it works against are a matter of wealth.

The fourth dynamic to notice is that the rights of the residents of Lancaster County, including the ones arrested for their protest, were irrelevant to the legal permitting of the pipeline. Because they had no property interest in the land, the protesters had no "standing" before the law to have their grievances heard about safety, aesthetics, lost historic significance of disturbed Native American burial grounds in the path of the pipeline, and other perceived harms. Their only legal status was that of trespassers on condemned land and nuisances to the pipeline workers. The law didn't represent their rights or interests.

The fifth dynamic to notice is that preserving the natural world did not factor into any of the legal proceedings. Nature is not a subject in the eyes of the law. It is an object, a collection of items to be owned and not a rights-bearing entity to be protected. If it is property, it may convey to the owner certain rights, but it has none itself.

Building Empire under the Radar: Because Nobody Wants to Say That's What's Going On

We need to untangle the braid of interacting rights in this case to understand where law begins and justice ends. My thesis is that federal constitutionalism serves wealth, not people and communities, and that the underlying logic used to rationalize this system of law and government is intrinsically and ethically flawed. To expose these flaws, let's start with a simple assertion: Ownership of specific property is not an unalienable right.

Not all of us are born equally advantaged with wealth. Unalienable rights are distributed equitably to all. We can be *voluntarily* alienated from our property, as through gifting, sale, or lease. We can also be *involuntarily* alienated from property through taxation, garnishment, condemnation (eminent domain), theft, and other means. Hence, property is *not* an unalienable right.

Sometimes, as in the assertion of eminent domain against the Adorers of the Blood of Christ, the enforcement of law reflects this fact. The tenuousness of the right to personal property is made very clear. But the law's deference to all sorts of rights in property is so integral to American constitutionalism that loss of property rights generally only occurs when the rights of one party conflict with the interests of another, wealthier party. Overriding this deference requires the full collaboration of government and wealth. In a conflict between personal property and privileged property, the law and court precedent favor privileged rights over personal rights. This is the big secret that everybody knows but no one talks about.

American law developed in a culture of colonial expansion. It intentionally protects the accumulation of privileged property (wealth). There is no wonder in this. Such accumulation is the engine of empire. Protection of personal property by law follows the logic of empire. Small fortunes may grow to larger ones, so they are to be protected. But that paternalism diverges from the absolute when doing so interferes with more effective means of acquiring and centralizing control over resources. Placing resources under the jurisdiction of law's authority is how empires are built and is the purpose of legal protections for amassed property. The authority and rights developed over the years for large business corporations have been magnified for no other purpose than to facilitate this acquisition and centralization of power.

There are inadequate enforceable rules for safeguarding the earned wages and assets of less affluent people against the juggernaut of commercial empires both large and small. Today's business corporation falls into both the large and small categories. Some are able to compete on a global scale, almost as nations without a land base. When law is used to protect the privileges of empire by declaring wealth and its uses exempt from public law and thus not responsible for harming the rights of individuals, communities, and the whole planet, then we are all are at risk.

The misapplication of eminent domain robs people of their certainty of justice, because to the average person property is property, and the law should not favor one possession over another. Like so many other confrontations between unalienable rights and rights vested in property, eminent domain exposes an undemocratic arrangement. An unacknowledged partnership exists between government and wealth in the guise of corporate power. The legalized expropriation of personal property, labor, public resources, and services when it benefits private accumulation of profit and wealth demonstrates what much of American law is all about.

The project of empire building is accomplished through legally sanctioned mechanisms for the appropriation of other people's property, labor, savings, and rights. The more primitive methods involve physical violence. Domestically, those means have been largely replaced by procedural violence inflicted through agencies, departments, authorities, and the maddening bureaucracy of the courts.

The official misuse of eminent domain is only the most blatant example of how rights vested in property rule over all other considerations. The personal right to property lodged in each natural person yields to the powers lodged in the privileged property of wealth and exercised through the courts. The conflict between personal property and privileged property is a battle in which unalienable rights arrive disarmed by law, which protects privileges vested in property.

Those who gain possession of privileged property can invade the larder of common rights through many doors. They gain entry through expropriation, appropriation, inheritance, rent-seeking,[2] usury,[3] garnishment,[4] seizure, assumption, trade, litigation, annexation, conquest . . . in fact, theft. Setting aside illegal and unscrupulous ways of achieving wealth, we can ask: "Is the accumulation of property by legal means an unalienable right?"

The answer has nothing to do with legality. It has to do with basic logic. Because privileged property can be increased, then the legal rights conveyed by it can be increased. If those rights are unalienable, then unalienable rights can be compounded. If so, we would have to conclude that some unalienable rights are not equal rights. By extension, because some people can have more unalienable rights than others, then some unalienable rights could be withheld legally from the majority or a disfavored minority. The concept of unalienable rights would then be meaningless. The more rational conclusion is that unalienable rights are in fact equal for all and that property is not an unalienable right.

Unalienable rights, unlike wealth, cannot be compounded. They are not able to be increased by accumulation. They cannot be purchased. But the rights conveyed by privileged property facilitate an exponential increase in the amount of deference law pays to people in possession of it. Wealth accumulation isn't just an increase in leisure and luxury. It represents a substantial decrease in rights for everyone else. A bias in the laws and Constitution of the US makes it so.

Over time, and under color of law, rights vested in property, which I'll shorthand as the *rights of property,* have eroded the natural rights of everyone but the propertied class. Rights conveyed to the wealthy through privileged property are prized above all others under American law. There is a reason. The Federalists, who insisted on a strong central government and not a democracy governed by We the People, had the building of a continental empire clearly in mind. They made provisions in the Constitution for the addition of new territories and states. They made other provisions to accelerate and defend minority ownership of most of the property, along with the control of lawmaking and governance by that same minority.

All of this is in sharp contrast to the aspirations of American revolutionaries and the expectations of newcomers to the United States. It's antithetical to the idealism celebrated in songs and parades on the Fourth of July. What we have is the antithesis of what we want. The reason more than two hundred communities in the United States have enacted local community bills of rights that challenge wealth-privileging legal doctrines is that people have begun to wake up from the sinister spell that insists this is the way it has to be.

Lines in the Sand: Property Is Ink on Paper

Let's ask the most basic question: Where does property come from?

From outer space, it's not possible to see national borders or property lines on the earth's surface. Our blue-green home doesn't look at all like a Rand-McNally atlas or a municipal plat. State and town boundaries are invisible. Property lines are undetectable.

So if property in land and political borders can't be seen empirically, where do they exist? The answer: They exist only in law and in the minds of people who believe that law reflects reality.[5]

To illustrate how "real property" becomes real in our heads, let me tell you a brief story about the colonization of the Western Hemisphere by Europeans. When Christopher Columbus returned from his exploratory venture to the Americas, he visited the monarchs of Portugal and Spain. Both kingdoms wished to claim the newly found lands for themselves. The dispute between them was settled by Pope Alexander VI. He drew a line on a crude map, from the North to the South Pole, and cut South America in two. He declared that to the east of the line, where present-day Brazil juts to the right into the Atlantic Ocean, Portugal would rule; to the west of that line, it would be Spain.

The pope's pen was as powerful as a magic wand. The spell he cast was slow to take hold, but the ink on that map changed the course of history. It had no immediate physical effect on the planet. Yet that ink had the indelible effect of creating a law-based rationale for invading conquistadors. Meanwhile, it left indigenous people by the millions, and the whole of the natural world, without rights and without protection. The Doctrine of Discovery espoused by Pope Alexander VI in his "Inter Caetera" papal bull of 1493 legalized conquest, plunder, and exploitation.

Justifying Injustice: The Emperor's Philosophers

Thirty-three years later, Francis Bacon published his *Novum Organum*, laying out the basis for scientific inquiry. He imagined that human beings could escape the limitations nature imposed on us by deducing its laws from observation. Where Pope Alexander VI drew a line and made a law that severed the physical world into parts and parcels, Bacon intended to dissect all of nature, own its secrets, and use *those* laws to similarly enrich whoever could command them. Bacon is quoted as saying: "My only earthly wish is . . . to stretch the deplorably narrow limits of man's dominion over the universe to their promised bounds . . . [Nature will be] bound into service, hounded in her wanderings and put on the rack and tortured for her secrets."[6]

The rituals of mechanical intervention into nature, like the pope's ritual of dividing up the planet into estates, made world-spanning conquest possible. "I am come in very truth leading you to Nature with all her children to bind her to your service and make her your slave," Bacon is purported to have said. "The mechanical inventions of recent years do not merely exert a gentle guidance over Nature's courses, they have the power to conquer and subdue her, to shake her to her foundations."[7] These comments summarize the imperial spirit of the age.

Now, in the twenty-first century, we begin to see how both humanity and nature have been shaken and the bonds of equality and community severed. The world has been reduced to a matrix of possessions held together by a tangle of laws defining who owns what (and who owns naught). The pope's ink on a map became a point of contagion for a political idea that now rules the world. The laws of possession separate the haves and the have-nots, making community into an atomized cloud of competition rather than a bond of mutual aid.

Similarly, Bacon's extraction of mechanical rules from nature has severed humanity from nature's community. The privatization of nature and other societies became the obsession of a culture experimenting with altering its place in the world. Many today predict a terrible endgame, when the laws of nature and human laws clash.

In the age of conquest, it was law as much as gunpowder that helped Europeans conquer whole continents. The law of boundaries, borders, enclosures, and property, armed with the distilled and lifeless laws of nature, had a hypnotic effect on European culture. A whole civilization was blinded to the horror and harm it would do.

No thought was given by Pope Alexander VI to the cascade of injustices his pen stroke would precipitate. The lives of the people already living in the lands he cavalierly assigned to Spain and Portugal were dismissed as irrelevant. There was no anticipation of the future clear-cutting of the Amazon jungle, the centuries of war, oppression, revolution, and sadness that the stroke of a pen would catalyze. The pontiff and his favored monarchs imagined only the wealth and power the lawful privatization of the Western Hemisphere would convey to them.

In the second volume of his work on inequality, Jean-Jacques Rousseau wrote that

> The first man who, having enclosed a piece of ground, bethought himself of saying This is mine, and found people

simple enough to believe him, was the real founder of civil society. From how many crimes, wars, and murders, from how many horrors and misfortunes might not any one have saved mankind, by pulling up the stakes, or filling up the ditch, and crying to his fellows: Beware of listening to this impostor; you are undone if you once forget that the fruits of the earth belong to us all, and the earth itself to nobody.[8]

Another philosopher, John Locke, wrote that "government has no other end, but the preservation of property."[9] A hundred years later, American revolutionaries such as Thomas Paine when he wrote *Common Sense* and Thomas Jefferson when he wrote the Declaration of Independence had other aspirations. For them the purpose of government is to secure unalienable rights, including the right to one's own labor and the product of it, and the right of the people to engage in self-government without deference to the priorities of wealth. But in America and in the nations around the globe whose social contract is rooted in conquest and colonialism, the ethics of power and possession prevailed.

Workers and the Law Serve Wealth

Understanding the distinction between personal property and privileged property is necessary to further illustrate why the accumulation of property is not an unalienable right. Going back to early American sources, we find Benjamin Franklin corresponding with the wealthiest man in the American colonies, the financier of the Revolution, Robert Morris. He wrote, "All the property that is necessary to a man for the conservation of the individual and the propagation of the species is his natural right, which none can justly deprive him of; but all property superfluous to such purposes is the property of the public, who by their laws have created it, and who may therefore by other laws dispose of it whenever the welfare of the public shall demand such a disposition."[10]

Let's be clear about whether there is a right to privileged property and where belief in that right comes from. Then let's ask if there is a right to one's personal property.

In all cases, law creates property. We aren't born with it. Whether it is the nuns' land and chapel in the woods or the pipeline company's commandeered right-of-way through their sanctuary, law and government decide who owns what. That goes for all types of property. Because all property exists subject to legal consent, law can either recognize a claim of ownership or deny it. What law cannot legitimately deny is the right to be free of servitude, where the fruit of one's labor belongs to another. What law cannot legitimately assert is that the value of the wages of servitude, in whole or in part, belongs to the master of the worker in pursuit of wealth. But, as we see, law readily and constantly does both. The Federalists who devised that law conflated the right of the wealthy to be free from community governance with the right of all people to be free of servitude. In further service to the opulent minority, the Federalists then denied freedom from servitude as a general right.

Let's consider the case of earned wages for work done. American law has acknowledged a right to be free from *involuntary* servitude, including but not limited to slavery, since adoption of the Thirteenth Amendment in 1865. Section 1 of the amendment says that "neither slavery nor involuntary servitude, except as a punishment for crime whereof the party shall have been duly convicted, shall exist within the United States, or any place subject to their jurisdiction."

Prior to adoption of that language into the Constitution, ownership of one's own labor was not recognized as a right.

Although hailed as the end of slavery in the United States, the Thirteenth Amendment didn't make freedom from involuntary servitude a recognized unalienable right. It allowed the enslavement of people convicted of crimes. With no cue from the amendment's language, judges have also decided that it allows government to impose involuntary military conscription on those unable to find a legal escape hatch.

We're examining the question of servitude to illustrate the difference between personal property and privileged property. The one, the right to own and control one's own labor—that is, the use of one's own body and mind to produce added value and thereby profit—is unalienable. It's not the added value, the property itself, that is unalienable. It's the liberty from labor for the benefit of another that is unalienable.

Liberty is one of three specific examples of unalienable rights mentioned in the Declaration of Independence. Servitude subtracts liberty from the person and is a direct violation of a fundamental right. But when rights are bestowed upon the property itself, as when corporate property becomes the repository of Bill of Rights protections, then law acts to protect additive acquisition (privileged property). It's that word *involuntary* that so clearly reveals that the Thirteenth Amendment was never intended to end the legal advantages of masters over workers, or to guarantee freedom from servitude as a constitutionally protected right. The essence of unalienable rights is that they cannot be separated from the person, not even voluntarily. By including the word "involuntary" in the amendment, servitude of poor people to wealthy people was preserved as a legally allowable arrangement.

Even though labor can no longer be stolen lawfully from a worker through enslavement, the laborer can still be persuaded to "voluntarily" waive rights to fair compensation in exchange for employment. The law allows it. What can be sold, surrendered, or volunteered is not by law unalienable. And thus, in the eyes of the law, freedom from servitude is not an unalienable right.

Accumulation of privileged property (wealth) requires the confiscation of value from the past and future industriousness of many others. Legalized servitude makes wealth possible. Possession of privileged property, such as a corporation, affords its owner the legal tools to protect wealth from redistribution by the community at large, from which the wealth flows.

Thus law creates a one-way gated pump for work converted into added value to flow away from its human producers and into privileged property, from which only the propertied minority is authorized to withdraw.

Legal scholar Morris R. Cohen wrote,

> The character of property as sovereign power compelling service and obedience may be obscured for us in a commercial economy by the fiction of the so-called labour contract as a free bargain and by the frequency with which service is rendered indirectly through a money payment. But . . . there [is] actually little freedom to bargain on the part of the steelworker or miner who needs a job . . . Today I do not directly serve my landlord if I wish to live in the city with a roof over my head, but I must work for others to pay him rent with which he obtains the personal services of others. The money needed for purchasing things must for the vast majority be acquired by hard labour and disagreeable service to those to whom the law has accorded dominion over the things necessary for subsistence.[11]

Once personal constitutional protections are waived by private contract, public law and the protections of the Bill of Rights are powerless to intervene. The employee may be required to surrender freedoms of speech, assembly, privacy, and religion, and other rights on the job as a contractual condition of employment. Each unalienable right becomes alienable. Each conditional right becomes moot. Rights of persons are made subordinate to rights in corporate property. Private law (as noted earlier, law related to contracts and corporations) is given deference over public law (which sets policies and places sanctions on anti-social behavior. It deals with issues of general concern to the community at-large). Minority interests trump general rights.

The worker's right to wages is limited and maxed out by whatever minimum wage (or lack thereof) is set in his or her political jurisdiction. Beyond that nominal regulation, the employer and not the worker or the law decides whether that right includes a paycheck adequate to cover the necessities of life. Ownership of privileged property gives the employer this power to decide.

When the worker's income is taxed, there's no assurance that his or her priorities will be represented in budgeting how the collected revenue will be spent. Often, the portion of wages taken by government will serve the interests of the employer and others similarly in possession of privileged property, and not those of the worker. There is no inherent reason for this. There is a bias in the law. A viable economy would still be possible if unalienable rights took precedent over property amassed as wealth. Empire, however, might not be possible.

Unequal Protection: The Myth of Equality before the Law

Law creates property in all its forms by sanctioning its existence. But how the law treats personal property contrasts sharply with how it treats privileged property, as we are beginning to see.

The species of privileged property have proliferated unchecked for a century and a half through modification of the law. From simple interest on loans to compounding interest; from mineral rights to intellectual property rights; from "naming rights" to copyrights; from stocks and bonds to future profits; from proprietary rights to corporate rights; from legal standing to engineered legal precedent—the number of institutionalized legal privileges for wealth has expanded with no sign of stopping.

It matters how all of this is understood. Adam Winkler, professor of constitutional law at UCLA School of Law, has written an entertaining book titled *We the Corporations: How American Businesses Won Their Civil Rights*. The author tells the story from the droll perspective of victimized corporations struggling for justice and how they gained constitutional rights from the Supreme Court. He compares the pursuit of legal advantages for wealthy people and their corporate property to a civil rights movement. It is a clever device. But Winkler makes a more serious historical observation that, whereas it only required that the wealthy ask for those rights for their chartered property, it took decades of abolitionist struggles, a civil war, and three constitutional amendments to free African Americans from the status of rightless property.

A laughably baseless interpretation of the Fourteenth Amendment let the Supreme Court change corporate property into a person with constitutional protections that rival those afforded to real people. That was in 1886, thirty-four years before the Constitution was amended to recognize the right of women to vote. To this day, women lack an equal rights amendment. Corporations have been guaranteed equal rights with men under the Fourteenth Amendment for over a century.

The lesson here is that the American system of law ensures that wealth has access to the Supreme Court to protect its rights, whereas ordinary people have no automatic entrée into the halls of justice to secure their rights.

In the last pages of his book, Winkler tells the story of Mora County, New Mexico, and the Mora Community Water Rights and Self-Government Act of 2013. It's an ordinance I had a hand in drafting and shepherding to adoption at the request of community members and the county commissioner, John Olivas. Winkler holds our ordinance up as an example of how we might push back against the hegemony of wealth and the privatization of the federal Bill of Rights.

In a region where water is scarce and widespread hydraulic fracturing (fracking) was being proposed, county residents grew concerned. Fracking uses immense quantities of water to force natural gas out of the ground. In the process, the water is tainted with poisons and not reusable. That's what prompted them to contact CELDF and eventually enact their ordinance in 2013.

The county law declared that, because water is indispensable to life, it is an unalienable right. It declared the corporation's property interests in natural gas, its mineral rights, not to be unalienable. And it held that unalienable rights supersede the inferior rights in property.

Later that same year, the Independent Petroleum Institute of New Mexico and a couple of similarly interested individuals sued Mora County for adopting an ordinance banning the extraction of fossil fuels within the county. The lawsuit claimed that the ordinance violated the corporation's First, Fifth, and Fourteenth Amendment rights. It was a civil rights suit against the county.

It was all but preordained that without the overriding guidance of conscience and with a near-sacred sense of obligation to precedent, a judge would eventually overturn Mora's water rights ordinance as a violation of the civil rights of a corporation. And that's what happened. In federal district court, it was not the people's right to water but the mineral rights belonging to the corporate property and the corporate property's rights to free speech, due process, and equal protection of the law that prevailed.

There was no appeal. A well-funded political campaign to oust the commissioners who enacted the ordinance succeeded in replacing them with industry-friendly commissioners who walked away from the defense of the people's right to water.

Mora's ordinance is one of hundreds drafted by CELDF and enacted across the country. Wealth has deployed its arsenal of legal advantages against a few of them, punishing municipalities financially, even threatening to bankrupt them, while blaming CELDF for bringing grief and costly litigation upon them. Lower courts, unwilling to make decisions about constitutional issues, generally rely on such mechanisms as state preemption to safeguard the interests of property and wealth. Federal courts lean on Supreme Court precedent to protect the civil rights previously bestowed on corporate property.

One of the successes we've come to expect from campaigns like the one in Mora is the exposure of the legal substructure that arms the priorities of wealth with power to neutralize the unalienable rights of people. That may not seem like much of a win, but in the context of public obliviousness to the true nature of American law, it is a necessary first step toward building a community rights movement.

The Land Must Be Liberated: Emancipating the Planet

The community rights movement into which you are being invited conceives of a much more inclusive definition of *com-*

munity than the framers of the US Constitution had in mind. For them, white men who own property were the legitimate rulers of the nation. Women, Native Americans, African Americans, paupers of all sorts had no place in the governance of the community or the nation. It's time to open the gated fortress where people and their possessions separate themselves from nature, fellow human beings, and responsibility to them, smug in their presumed superiority. We can reconstitute community as it should exist: people living in harmony with nature, rather than as parasites.

Nature is the greater community, and we are a part of it.

We are not helpless to begin the task of correcting and making amends for the cultural, genocidal, and ecocidal errors of the past. Or if we are, then the visceral longing for freedom and real justice and preservation of the planet are lost causes. But that is an intolerable outcome.

Liberating the planet from those who claim to own it must coincide with liberating We the People and all of us in nature from the dictatorship of property. These inextricably interwoven causes have the same goal: right relationship and true freedom.

In 2006, I was working with clients in the borough of Tamaqua in Schuylkill County, Pennsylvania. It's anthracite coal country, where a century and a half of mining has left the landscape pockmarked with holes and rubble and a shallow-rooted forest of perpetual saplings that will never become full-grown trees. Once the Industrial Revolution switched from coal to petroleum for most of its energy, the same communities from which natural "resources" had been stripped became the dumping ground for toxic waste. Gaping strip mines and deep mine shafts were eyed for "reclamation," meaning they'd be filled with industrial waste, coal fly ash, urban sewage solids, and river dredge.

The people of Tamaqua thought that was a bad idea. I worked with them to draft a local law that included provisions my colleagues and I had been developing for a few years. At the heart of the ordinance was this concept: Unalienable rights come first.

As we worked on the draft ordinance, I had a conversation with Cathy Miorelli, a member of the borough council and full-time school nurse. She wasn't concerned that the draft law for the little town would take on the "well-established" constitutional rights of the Lehigh Coal and Navigation Corporation and the preemptive authority of the Commonwealth of Pennsylvania. No. She went to the heart of the matter and raised the issue of property rights. How could Tamaqua prohibit landowners from doing whatever they want with their property, to the point of creating serious hazards for the community? She knew the reverence for property central to American law. How could we challenge such a foundational doctrine?

It wasn't a question. It was a challenge. "No, really: How can we do it?"

As it turned out, CELDF's executive director, Thomas Linzey; our historian and mentor, Richard Grossman; and I had been having quiet, internal conversations about an idea that was raised in the 1970s by Christopher Stone, professor of law at the University of Southern California, in his book *Should Trees Have Standing?* Its subtitle was *Toward Legal Rights for Natural Objects.* Professor Stone asked how society could really protect the environment when nature has been subdivided into privatized parcels. Under Western law, ecosystems and nature have but one legal status: that of property. Owners of property have few enforceable obligations to others when it comes to how they treat their property. If only nature had legal rights of its own, Stone mused; then maybe something could be done to protect it.

And that is what Cathy Miorelli was curious about. What could be done to stop the owner of the Springdale coal mine from filling it with toxins? Up to that point, no one had taken Christopher Stone's question seriously enough to test it. So, we did.

On September 19, 2006, Tamaqua became the first government on earth to recognize legally enforceable rights for ecosystems. Section 7.6 of the ordinance states:

> It shall be unlawful for any corporation or its directors, officers, owners, or managers to interfere with the existence and flourishing of natural communities or ecosystems, or to cause damage to those natural communities and ecosystems. The Borough of Tamaqua, along with any resident of the Borough, shall have standing to seek declaratory, injunctive, and compensatory relief for damages caused to natural communities and ecosystems within the Borough, regardless of the relation of those natural communities and ecosystems to Borough residents or the Borough itself. Borough residents, natural communities, and ecosystems shall be considered to be "persons" for purposes of the enforcement of the civil rights of those residents, natural communities, and ecosystems.

It was a first. The law still stands, not having been challenged with corporate or state litigation. Lehigh Coal and Navigation Company did not go forward with its dumping plans. It cannot be said that the ordinance or this new approach to protecting the environment won the day once and for all. But it did gain international attention.

By now the rights of nature have become something of a cause célèbre. Beneath the legal fight to protect the planet and its living systems is a battle to the death—or to life—over legal rights in property and the status of nature in the eyes of the law. Word of what Tamaqua had done traveled far and abroad. For those who doubt that what we do locally in our hometowns can have any important or lasting effect, take note.

Following news of Tamaqua's brave leap into uncharted territory, Ecuador recruited CELDF staff to guide their Constitutional Assembly in drafting a key part of what would become their new national constitution. They wanted to include rights for Pachamama—Mother Earth. By popular vote in 2010, with overwhelming support, Ecuador's new national constitution recognizing fundamental legal rights for nature became its new law of the land. The English translation of the constitutional provision on which my colleagues worked says this: "Natural communities and ecosystems possess the unalienable right to exist, flourish, and evolve within Ecuador. Those rights shall be self-executing, and it shall be the duty and right of all Ecuadorian governments, communities, and individuals to enforce those rights."

What Tamaqua had done, and what Ecuador did, became an example for bold American communities and nation-states around the globe. Readers may be familiar with the changed legal status of nature and natural systems in New Zealand, Bolivia, India, Colombia, and elsewhere. Here in the US, through our community rights organizing, we've added the rights of nature to all the local laws we draft for American communities.

The "no fracking" Community Bill of Rights enacted by Pittsburgh in 2010 recognized the rights of ecosystems, saying: "Natural communities and ecosystems, including, but not limited to, wetlands, streams, rivers, aquifers, and other water systems, possess inalienable and fundamental rights to exist and flourish within the City of Pittsburgh. Residents of the City shall possess legal standing to enforce those rights on behalf of those natural communities and ecosystems."

Our associate director, Mari Margil, has traveled the globe to help officials and activists develop rights-of-nature legislation and constitutional provisions. We were not involved in New Zealand's settling with the aboriginal Maori people to recognize legal rights for the Wanganui River. The movement for nature's rights has begun to take on a life of its own.

Here in the US, more than forty cities, municipalities, and counties have enacted laws recognizing nature as a rights-bearing entity. No longer mere property in which special privileges are stored, later to be enjoyed by its human owners, nature is recognized in those communities as fully qualified to enjoy its own rights and to have them defended in court.

The reason that nature needs recognition for her legal rights is *not* that nature should be considered a legal person. We've changed our understanding and approach since our first venture into unalienable rights of nature in Tamaqua. Nature is not a human being. And it's not a mere "juristic person," or corporation. It has its own priorities and deserves and needs these protections because Western law and the rule of property treat nature as the slave of its many owners.

It is the privilege to destroy that makes the owners of land and "resources" dangerous to life on earth. The rest of us, who do not "own" the world, have unalienable rights, including the right to withdraw presumed privileges of property ownership when they threaten others' rights and do harm to the world. The privilege to destroy is among the cache of governing powers conveyed to landowners by the rights *of* property. It has brought to the world the climate crisis, a mass species die-off, and the ecocide of the oceans, not to mention the proliferation of disease, dislocation, misery, and suffering for people and life in general. To argue that the community has no authority to bring this carnage to an end is a blithe absurdity.

There is no doubt that making the needed changes to privileges associated with property will be one of our culture's greatest challenges. Freeing nature from bondage to its "owners" will alter the meaning of the word *property* in ways that will defy centuries of institutionalized privilege for those who possess the lion's share of everything. The propertied class will resist any change that diminishes their dominion over us and the entire living world. They will employ uninformed friends, family, and strangers as their armed workforce to resist our efforts. They will engage in propaganda and misinformation, name-calling, villainization, and criminalization of our efforts, our gatherings, even our thoughts, to stop us from wresting total control from them. The stakes could not be higher. To lose is to lose everything. Your help is needed in this struggle for survival.

CHAPTER TWO

The Ongoing Counterrevolution

The uniformity of the Framers' economic status had a predictable impact on the Constitution. It provides protections for property rights and limits the political powers of the poor. In contrast, it does not provide for the needs of the lower classes. Instead, those provisions focused on the poor are designed to suppress insurrections, to prohibit state debtor relief laws, and to prevent property redistributions.

—Ann M. Burkhart

Where Do Rights Reside: In People or in Property?

Until the American Revolution, the proprietorship colony of Pennsylvania was run by a General Assembly overseen by the descendants of William Penn. It was made up of Quaker members of the commercial elite. They opposed independence because of their business dealings with England, and without Pennsylvania on board, other states refused to endorse secession from the empire.

Only wealthy white men were represented in the General Assembly, and as in most of the colonies, voting and holding office were open only to white men with substantial property. That left out most men and everyone else.

Thanks to some backroom chicanery by Sam and John Adams, Benjamin Franklin, and Doctor Benjamin Rush, unbanked men from the rural countryside gathered and descended on the State House in Philadelphia, where both the Pennsylvania General Assembly and the Continental Congress were meeting. The rabble tossed out their colonial betters when those men refused to send delegates with instructions to support a declaration of independence. The insurgents voted in their own representatives to the General Assembly, and they quickly put Pennsylvania on the side of independence. With Pennsylvania on board, the scales tipped in the Continental Congress in favor of separation from England. Then the propertyless assembly got busy writing the first constitution of the commonwealth of Pennsylvania.

When they gathered to draft their 1776 state constitution, the rabble-run General Assembly decided to break with British tradition and allow all men—white and black—to vote and hold office, whether they were rich or poor. Benjamin Franklin was instrumental in crafting that early state constitution.

To justify dropping property qualifications, he told this story. "Today a man owns a jackass worth fifty dollars and he is entitled to vote; but before the next election the jackass dies. The man in the meantime has become more experienced, his knowledge of the principles of government, and his acquaintance with mankind, are more extensive, and he is therefore better qualified to make a proper selection of rulers—but the jackass is dead, and the man cannot vote. Now gentlemen, pray inform me, in whom is the right of suffrage? In the man or in the jackass?"[1]

This story is a very clear illustration of how law vests the right to govern within property, not men. The jackass is the most rudimentary example of privileged property. Franklin's anecdote is worth keeping in mind as we consider less obvious forms of privileged property. For instance, when we turn to constitutional mechanisms such as the commerce clause, it may become clearer how wealth arms law to stand against democracy.

When wealth allows its owner to engage in commerce across state borders, the owner is freed from local and state regulation of commercial activities. The commerce clause forbids state and local lawmaking to regulate the exchange of goods, services, and finance across state lines. Interfering with wealth's extraterritorial reach, regardless of its impact locally, is thus prohibited.

How the commerce clause and other constitutional mechanisms infringe on the people's right of self-government will become clear as we consider real-life examples of how rights in property exempt the wealthy from public governance while at the same time empowering the wealthy to enforce legal protections of their publicly injurious projects against democratic interference. But before we zip too quickly into current events, let's have another look at how, in the past, public rights were crudely privatized and vested in property, and how governing was made the exclusive privilege of those owning wealth.

IN 1841–1842, a little-known civil war was fought in Rhode Island, called the Dorr War. At that time, Rhode Island was the last state to require ownership of land as a condition of voting, holding office, and participating in governance. The followers of Thomas Dorr, who led the rebellion against the state, held their own constitutional convention and created a competing state government during the uprising.

To justify adopting their People's Constitution in defiance of the state legislature and without following the rules that let only landowners participate in amending the constitution, they published a note from "the Nine Lawyers." One of their arguments for the invalidity of the old constitution, from which the "freemen" (landowners) benefited because they maintained the suffrage by right of land ownership, was that the American Revolution took sovereignty away from the king and gave it to the people as a whole. "[I]t held that the sovereign power of a State is the power which prescribes the form of government; in Rhode Island, at the Revolution, it passed to the whole people; for, if to a part, the owners of land, then it really passed to the soil itself."[2]

As with Franklin's jackass, the right to vote was vested in property and could be claimed only by those who came into possession of it. It could as easily be lost by separation from the property. By that logic, the freemen of Rhode Island received their political freedom from the property they owned. Anyone could partake of sovereignty by buying or inheriting land. Self-government was not an unalienable right inherent in human beings but a privilege set aside, awaiting the arrival of whoever could wrest possession of the land or its riches from the rest of the community.

In the end, the unbanked and underbanked rebels were defeated. They didn't get to keep their revolutionary constitution. Thomas Dorr, no longer governor of the shadow government, fled and went into hiding. A year later, he returned and was charged with treason and sentenced to solitary confinement. But it was not an utter defeat. Both the authorized and the shadow governments had appealed to the federal government to intervene. President John Tyler decided not to takes sides. And in 1843, the state created a new constitution that dropped the property requirements for white men born in the country. That same year, Thomas Dorr was granted a pardon. He died later in the year.

With the end of the Dorr War, the civil rights struggle of propertyless white men came to an end in the United States.

The achievement of "universal manhood suffrage" disarmed the propertied class of one of the weapons it had deployed against democracy. Despite that setback, vesting sovereign governing rights in property was just getting off the ground. It would evolve into the most powerful political and social tool ever defined in law.

The Enclosure of the Commons: Today We Call It Privatization

It will be wise to remind ourselves of the history of the British enclosures. It is emblematic of the transference of public rights from the majority into the private possession of a privileged minority. The enclosures in England ended traditional rights in land. From the seventeenth through the nineteenth centuries, the enclosure movement took land that had formerly been shared in common by all and changed it to privately owned land, always with words on paper to document the appropriation.

The English government and aristocracy justified the enclosing of land with claims that large fields could be farmed more efficiently than individual plots. Some claimed that putting an end to subsistence farming and consolidating land and control would yield great commercial benefits. Similar claims about "efficiencies of scale" continue to be made today to rationalize the corporatization of agriculture and the privatization of schools and medicine in the United States.

It wasn't only farmland that was privatized and expropriated from communities under the British enclosures. According to historians Linebaugh and Rediker, "at the end of the fifteenth century, when water was drawn to London through wooden pipes . . . the Fellowship of the Brotherhood of Saint Christopher of the Waterbearers of London did most of the hauling from the conduits. Water was free. In 1581 this changed as the first privately owned, pumped water supply was constructed at the London Bridge. 'We have water companies now instead of water carriers,' wrote Johnson in 1598. By the 1660s the era of free water by right had ended—another commons expropriated."[3]

Today the "efficiencies" of privatization are noticeably calculated without regard to harms inflicted on society and the planet. Opposing the enclosures today means taking unalienable rights seriously and acting on the premise that our communities have not only full authority but a duty to protect those rights.

In 2008, THE PEOPLE behind the corporate property known as the Nestlé Corporation quietly sank twenty-three test wells in a supposedly protected forest in the New Hampshire town of Nottingham. When the wells were discovered, community members pulled together and planned at their annual town meeting to do something about it. For a few months, they worked behind the scenes with the help of Gail Darrell, CELDF's New Hampshire community rights organizer, to draft an ordinance that would stop Nestlé from moving forward with plans to privatize the town aquifer for a water-bottling operation.

The ordinance was enacted overwhelmingly by a show of hands at the town meeting. It was titled the Nottingham Water Rights and Local Self-Government Ordinance. Among other declarations in the preamble, it states,

> We the people of Nottingham declare that all of our water is held in the public trust as a common resource to be used for the benefit of Nottingham residents and of the natural ecosystems of which they are a part. We believe that the cor-

poratization of water supplies in this community—placing the control of water in the hands of a corporate few, rather than the community—would constitute tyranny and usurpation . . . [D]uty requires us to recognize that two centuries' worth of governmental conferral of constitutional powers upon corporations has deprived people of the authority to govern their own communities and requires us to take affirmative steps to remedy that usurpation of governing power.

The ordinance prohibited corporations from extracting groundwater within the town as a protection of the people's unalienable right to water, which is essential to life. Before long, the surreptitiously installed test wells were removed. Direct democracy prevailed for the moment.

In other towns across the continent, the same water extraction issue arises frequently. And there are many other instances of concentrated wealth exploiting communities and violating their rights. National and state land reserves are being opened to clear-cutting, oil and gas extraction, and strip mining.[4] Municipal authorities, once part of the public domain, are being gutted, their mandate to serve public needs converted into tools for private profit. Echoes of the enclosure of the commons in Britain accompany the march to privatize the public sector in the United States. Meanwhile, the community rights movement has been busy dismantling official rationalizations for laws that protect corporate property and wealthy investors from community attempts at self-preservation.

THE SAME BRITISH MERCHANT class that kicked traditional residents off privatized land during the enclosures prevailed on Parliament to make it illegal to be "landless and masterless." Vagabonds faced imprisonment and indentureship, and whole families were delivered into bondage. The dispossessed of England, Scotland, and Ireland provided unpaid labor for expansion of the empire. Many were forced to serve wealthy masters in far-off lands and to labor without rights in the new colonies.

When the supply of dispossessed Irish and Scottish paupers who'd been "barbadosed" to the colonies for their free labor was not enough, the empire began transporting kidnapped Africans to its colonies. Although England had no legal precedent for treating human beings as property, and although the central government strictly forbade its colonies from lawmaking for the benefit of settlers, the Caribbean colonies were permitted to develop a body of law that defined African slaves as a new kind of property.

South African author Ronald Segal wrote,

> The colonial legislatures, though subject to the imperial government, were left largely free to make laws for which there were no counterparts in Britain and which were designed specifically to deal with the status and management of slaves. The colonial codes were based on the contention that blacks . . . constituted property . . . Legislators employed the very value of liberty . . . in a form of reverse moral leverage, so that it applied only to the rights of proprietorship and excluded even such rights for the slave as Roman law had allowed in conceding that slaves were people as well as property.[5]

The rudiments of the rights *of* property were being developed even before there was a United States of America. Those new laws extended greater privileges to a minority of slave-holding commercial aristocrats. The sacred status of law had the uncanny effect of beguiling them to believe that their privileges were wholesome and for the best.

The land-rich men of colonial North America would have been familiar with this history of enclosure of public land and confiscation of human labor. The diverse faction of wealthy men known to history as the Federalists would create a compromise constitution between northern manufacturers and merchants and the southern slavocracy. In that new frame of government, they would pioneer a new sort of enclosure that privatized public law and government.

Mad Tom: Thomas Paine in the Royal Neck

Thomas Paine proposed a system for remedying the oppressions of the enclosures. Paine was a radical thinker and questioned everything from the legitimacy of the British monarchy and the beneficence of organized religion to the justification for the American colonies remaining part of the empire.

In January 1776, Thomas Paine published his pamphlet titled *Common Sense*. In clear, simple language, he explained the absurdity of aristocratic government. He argued for independence from the British Empire and establishment of a government based on securing rights for all. The British press skewered the commoner Paine with political caricatures and named him "Mad Tom" or "the Man of Rights."

Common Sense became an immediate best seller. Just six months later, Paine's views on unalienable rights inspired dozens of communities to send delegates to the Continental Congress demanding a break with Britain. Thomas Jefferson soon got his commission to write the Declaration of Independence.

Paine also wrote a lesser-known pamphlet called *Agrarian Justice*, which proposed a reversal of the injustices brought about by the enclosure of the commons. He understood the expropriation of land under color of law to be no more than rationalized theft. He had no tolerance for romanticizing imperial conquest as the "spread of civilization." In his opening remarks, he wrote: "Whether that state that is proudly, perhaps erroneously, called civilization, has most promoted or most injured the general happiness of man, is a question that may be strongly contested. On one side the spectator is dazzled by splendid appearances; on the other, he is shocked by extremes of wretchedness; both of which he has erected. The most affluent and the most miserable of the human race are to be found in the countries that are called civilized."[6]

Paine went further to say, "Man did not make the earth, and, though he had a natural right to occupy it, he had no right to locate as his property in perpetuity any part of it; neither did the creator of the earth open a land office, from whence the first title-deeds should issue."

But Paine understood that there is a legitimate sense in which rights can be attached to land. He tells his readers that he intentionally titled his essay *Agrarian Justice* and not *Agrarian Law* because common rights to the earth were tempered when humans turned from nomadic lives to cultivating the soil. He claimed that "landed property began . . . from the impossibility of separating the improvement made by cultivation, from the earth itself . . . till, in the end, the common right of all became confounded into the cultivated rights of the individual."[7]

Paine defended both the rights of the people living communally on the land and the rights of those who cultivated the land and thereby added social value to it. He said that all members of the community had been "thrown out of their natural inheritance," including the ones who cultivated the land. "But the landed monopoly that began with [cultivation], has produced the greatest evil." He then proposed a solution that would compensate the community for loss of land to the cultivators through enclosure, saying, "In advocating the case of the persons thus dispossessed, it is a right, and not a charity, that I am pleading for."

To pay the rest of the community reparations for their common rights in land lost to cultivation and inseparable from the cultivated fields, Paine proposed a national fund. Out of this fund, every person, rich or poor, would be paid a certain sum at the age of twenty-one, and then at the age of fifty would continue to receive an annual sum, in compensation.

The monies for this national fund would originate "at the moment that property is passing by the death of one person to the possession of another. In this case, the bequeather gives nothing: the receiver pays nothing. The only matter to him is, that the monopoly of natural inheritance, to which there never was a right, begins to cease in his person."[8]

Paine saw his proposed national fund as a reasonable way to make amends for the loss of our common natural inheritance of the earth and yet preserve the rights attached to personal property and the individual labor involved in cultivation.

Today's apologists for amassed wealth seethe at the notion of an inheritance tax. They call it a "death tax" and promote that language to falsely accuse its promoters of stealing from the dead and from their children. Their unreasoned belief that property is an inherent and inheritable right, and that those with much owe nothing to the rest, conveniently ignores the pedigree of plunder and privilege from which those riches spring.

With Paine's revolutionary *Common Sense* and *Agrarian Justice* in mind, it is worth noticing that there are no monuments to Paine in the nation's capital. He is not generally included in the pantheon of the nation's "founding fathers." No bust adorns the Capitol Rotunda. No memorials have been erected on the Mall or near Jefferson's Tidal Basin memorial. He's not even on coins or paper money. In fact, in 1949, as hysteria over Soviet communist infiltration of American politics took hold, according to historian Peter Linebaugh, "the FBI ordered the removal from public libraries of Howard Fast's influential wartime biographical novel, *Citizen Tom Paine,* as well as his one-volume selection of Paine's Works."[9]

"I Cannot Tell a Lie": Washington's Hidden Agenda

The contrast between the attitudes about property in land between the revolutionary Tom Paine and Federalist George Washington, "father of our country," could not be starker. Washington treated neither commoners under his military command nor squatters on land he claimed to own with much paternal concern. He acquired much of his land holdings by buying up promissory notes issued to colonial infantrymen during the French and Indian War. The land grants were issued by the Virginia House of Burgesses in payment for their military service. Before the Revolution, those lands were part of the Virginia colony, and Washington was a member of the House.

Washington urged his men to sell the notes to him because he said the script was unlikely to be honored after the war. The soldiers, short on hard currency, had little choice but to surrender their claims. But contrary to Washington's allegation, the House of Burgesses *did* honor the script at the end of the war. His fortune seemed assured.

Whatever motivated Washington to throw in with the American revolutionaries to wage war on Britain, part of the calculation must certainly have been the Royal Proclamation of 1763. With it, King George III revoked land grants west of the Appalachian Mountains, to make peace with Native Americans and avoid the expense of military protection for settlers. As a result, Washington's property claims were rendered worthless while the British ruled.

The fate of Washington's land claims would rise or fall on the success or failure of the Revolution. With victory in hand, he employed agents to secure his claims. They evicted homesteading dirt farmers who had cleared land and built homes. Then Washington put plans in motion to open his frontier holdings to the extraction of resources by building a canal.[10]

James Madison, George Washington, and a cadre of fellow investors were itching for a man-made waterway that would open the frontier. They each had claims to large swaths of land in what is now western Pennsylvania and eastern Ohio. Their proposed canal would run parallel to the Potomac River along the Maryland and Virginia border.

To build it, they needed permission from the people of both states to charter a corporation that would oversee and finance the project. The Articles of Confederation reserved the chartering of corporations to each of the state legislatures. Washington and his partners would have to get the approval of Virginia and Maryland for the proposed Potomac Company to become a reality.

Chartering corporations was not taken lightly. The Revolution had been waged as much against the empire's largest chartered corporation, the British East India Company, as against the empire itself. It was the East India Company's tea that was famously dumped in Boston Harbor. If the Potomac venture was to succeed, both states would have to independently agree to enact legislation chartering the desired company.

It took ten years for the Potomac Company investors to receive the go-ahead from both states. The entrepreneurs resented the inconvenience—so much so that they hatched a counter-revolutionary plot to overturn the first constitution and remove democratic control of commercial activities from state and local governments.

The investors met in 1785 at Washington's Mount Vernon slave plantation. Their private discussions led to a decision to invite delegates from all the states to a convention the next year, to be held in Annapolis, Maryland. The reason they gave for the meeting was to consider a uniform system of commercial regulation "for their common interest and their permanent harmony." In 1786, they were disappointed to have delegates arrive from only five states: New York, New Jersey, Pennsylvania, Delaware, and Virginia attended.

The Annapolis delegates drafted a note to Congress requesting that a convention be called for the following spring to consider improvements to the Articles of Confederation that would cover more than just commercial trade. Congress obliged, and on February 21, 1787, adopted a resolution that read: "That in the opinion of Congress, it is expedient, that on the second Monday in May next, a convention of delegates, who shall have been appointed by the several states, be held at Philadelphia, for the sole and express purpose of revising the Articles of Confederation, and reporting to Congress and the several legislatures, such alterations and provisions therein, as shall, when agreed to in Congress, and confirmed by the states, render the federal constitution adequate to the exigencies of government, and the preservation of the union."[11]

Historian Robert L. Schuyler commented that "it turned out that in sanctioning the Philadelphia Convention the old congress was in effect signing its own death warrant."[12]

Seventy delegates to the 1787 Philadelphia convention were appointed by the state legislatures, although Rhode Island declined to participate. Fifty-five of the appointed delegates made an appearance. The invitation didn't mention the Federalist's plans to dispose of the revolutionary Articles of Confederation. Other than the counterrevolutionary conspirators, those who came were expecting to revise the Articles of Confederation.

By the end of the convention, only thirty-nine signed and recommended their handiwork to the states for ratification. The fourteen who declined to sign, along with those who chose not to attend, including Richard Henry Lee, Patrick Henry, Thomas Jefferson, Samuel Adams, and John Hancock, are among the notable Anti-Federalists who opposed ratification of the Federalists' document.

The Constitution Makes Public Law Private Property

James Madison arrived in Philadelphia with a draft for a completely new form of government, called the Virginia Plan. It became the blueprint for the constitution that would replace the Articles. He had competition from Alexander Hamilton, who arrived with his New York Plan. It proposed a limited monarchy.

Madison kept notes of the deliberations and recorded Hamilton's comments this way:

> I believe the British government forms the best model the world ever produced . . . It is admitted that you cannot have a good executive upon a democratic plan. See the excellency of the British executive . . . And let me observe, that an executive is less dangerous to the liberties of the people when in office during life . . . I confess that this plan and that from Virginia are very remote from the idea of the people . . . But the people are gradually ripening in their opinions of government—they begin to be tired of an excess of democracy.[13]

According to Madison's notes, John Dickinson of Pennsylvania believed "A limited Monarchy [is] one of the best Governments in the world . . . A limited Monarchy however was out of the question. The spirit of the times—the state of our affairs, forbade the experiment, if it were desirable."[14]

In 1788, Madison confessed that "among those who embraced the Constitution, there were, no doubt, some who were openly or secretly attached to monarchy and aristocracy."

But there were no claims to noble birth among the colonial gentry. Charles Cotesworth Pinckney of South Carolina remarked that he did "not suppose that in the confederation, there are one hundred gentlemen of sufficient fortunes to establish a nobility . . . If we have any distinctions, they may be divided into three classes. 1. Professional men. 2. Commercial men. 3. The landed interest. The latter is the governing power of America, and the other two must ever be dependent on them."[15]

So it was that land became the first species of privileged property. The constitutional counterrevolutionaries agreed among themselves that property in land, and in all the resources to be derived from it, would be the best measure of the legitimacy of a man's claim to membership in the governing class.

In the end, due to the "spirit of the times" as Dickinson put it, the Federalists decided not to institute a monarchy, and instead made wealth king. They accepted Madison's Virginia Plan as their starting point and then haggled over the details through the sweltering summer.

Eleven years earlier, however, Thomas Jefferson, inspired by Thomas Paine, had written eloquently in the Declaration of Independence that "We hold these truths to be self-evident, that all men are created equal, that they are endowed by their Creator with certain unalienable Rights."

In the spirit of those revolutionary times, he altered the usual triumvirate of Enlightenment-era rights typically listed as "life, liberty and property," replacing "property" with "the pursuit of happiness." It was this language and not the rhetoric of the Federalists that mobilized commoners to take up arms and risk their lives for independence from Britain.

The aspirations of commoners who fought for liberty from the empire were abandoned when George Washington, James Madison, Alexander Hamilton, Robert Morris, and other wealthy Federalists crafted the current US Constitution. Edmund Randolph of Virginia commented that the purpose for overturning the first constitution was "to provide a cure for the evils under which the U.S. labored; that in tracing these evils to their origin every man [present at the convention] had found it in the turbulence and follies of democracy."[16]

The thirty-nine delegates who were motivated to sign off on the Constitution at the end of the convention agreed that the country could live without venerating royal privileges, but they concluded that reverence for a wealthy landowning class, to which they all belonged, was indispensable to good governance.

They were well on their way to enthroning wealth as the repository of the right to govern.

✧ **CHAPTER THREE** ✧

Of Laws and Men

*Property and sovereignty, as every student knows, belong to
entirely different branches of the law. Sovereignty is a concept
of political or public law and property belongs to civil or private law. This distinction between public and private law is a
fixed feature of our law-school curriculum. It was expressed
with characteristic eighteenth-century neatness and clarity by
Montesquieu, when he said that by political laws we acquire
liberty and by civil law property, and that we must not apply
the principles of one to the other.*

—Morris R. Cohen

Protecting the Minority of the Opulent against the Majority

John Adams argued that the United States is "a government
of laws, and not of men."[1] What laws? Well, the ones he and
the propertied class devised. They would govern the new nation down through the years.

Adams had no faith in democracy. He trusted that the better men of society would rule well if their affairs were unhin-
dered by a majority with other priorities. "Democracy never
lasts long. It soon wastes, exhausts and murders itself. There
was never a democracy that did not commit suicide," he remarked.[2] Like his fellow Federalists, he counted himself among
the wise. "Thanks to God that he gave me stubbornness when

I know I am right," he wrote to Edmund Jennings five years before the Constitution was composed in Philadelphia.

The Federalists were not authorized by "the people" to secretly deliberate over the text of a new constitution. Their wealth-protecting purpose did not reflect the general will of the people, and they knew it. What of it? wondered an indifferent James Madison at the Philadelphia convention. In his notes of Tuesday, June 12, 1787, he quoted his own comments to his peers, saying, "if the opinions of the people were to be our guide, it would be difficult to say what course we ought to take. No member of the convention could say what the opinions of his Constituents were at this time . . . We ought to consider what was right and necessary in itself for the attainment of a proper Government."

The delegates may not have known the opinions of their constituents, but they hadn't bothered to ask. Unsurprisingly, the Federalists diligently protected wealth from redistribution by peasant revolutionaries. They preserved English common law and made legal precedent into a judicial insurance policy against redistribution of what once had belonged to no one.

Sir William Blackstone, the noted legal scholar of English common law, wrote that "so great is the regard of the law for private property, that it will not authorize the least violation of it; no, not even for the common good of the whole community."[3]

Precedent, when preserving this level of reverence for property, is nothing more than the *rule of property* weaponized into a persistent legal tradition guaranteeing that "decisions under which property rights have been acquired will not be overruled, though erroneous."[4] Precedent became the most reliable weapon in property's arsenal once the Constitution and its array of publicly enforceable private law became the law of the land.

Thomas Jefferson argued against importing English common law into the American legal code because it justified an unequal class structure that American revolutionaries had rejected. Jefferson's warnings went unheeded.

The Federalists were happy to retain the empire's common law—its judicial precedents—as an exegesis to the federal constitution. It added another layer of protection against "the excesses of democracy" that threatened to interfere with privileges for the wealthy. The scheme of government the Federalists proposed came as close to modeling the British system of lords and sirs as decorum would allow.

Hamilton reluctantly agreed to drop his openly elitist New York Plan that would have created a monarchy in all but name. He decided to back Madison's Virginia Plan. It proposed a less openly class-based constitution. It had the advantage of offering the superficial trappings of a republic that would be less objectionable to the masses. Hamilton commented that although the constitution thus framed would not establish the limited monarchy he preferred, the Virginia Plan would be "but pork still, with a little change of the sauce."[5]

Yet today there is a Broadway musical to the memory of Alexander Hamilton.

A century later, historian J. Allen Smith wrote that US law, by endowing property with the ability to convey rights, "has given to the minority a greater protection than it has enjoyed anywhere else in the world, save in those countries where the minority is a specially privileged aristocracy. This doctrine briefly stated is that property rights once granted are sacred and inviolable. A rigid adherence to this policy . . . would disregard the fact that vested rights are often vested wrongs. A government without authority to interfere with vested rights would have little power to promote the general welfare through legislation."[6]

Madison understood how the Constitution was being shaped to accommodate this change from a genealogical to a financial aristocracy. He addressed the convention saying, "in all civilized countries, the interests of a community will be divided. There will be debtors and creditors, and an unequal possession of property, and hence arises different views and different objects in government. This indeed is the groundwork of aristocracy; and we find it blended in every government, both ancient and modern. Even where titles have survived property, we discover the noble beggar haughty and assuming."[7]

The Federalists concluded at every turn that it is the possession of wealth, not lineage, that legitimizes aristocracy. Without riches, inherited aristocratic status was pathetic. Madison favored a system of government that on its surface respected no special status for any class. But he crafted one that put the power to govern into the hands of the wealthy.

By blocking popular participation, the new constitution ensured that all decisions would be left to the propertied citizens. At the convention in Philadelphia, Madison told the rest of the delegates that "if elections were open to all classes of people, the property of the landed proprietors would be insecure . . . [O]ur government ought to secure the permanent interests of the country against innovation. Landholders ought to have a share in the government, to support these invaluable interests, and to balance and check the other. They ought to be so constituted as to protect the minority of the opulent against the majority."[8]

In the mind of James Madison, and apparently others among the Federalists, "the permanent interests of the country" meant the interests of the propertied class.

The North American Free Trade Agreement of 1789

With Washington presiding over the convention, the Federalists from the northern states proposed a mechanism that would block commoners and their elected representatives from getting in the way of wealth accumulation and empire building. It comes down to these few words, known as the commerce clause: "[Congress shall have power] to regulate Commerce with foreign Nations, and among the several States, and with the Indian Tribes" (Article I, Section 8, Clause 3 of the US Constitution).

A constitutional prohibition against popular governance of interstate and international commerce comes later in the Constitution, where it says, "No State shall, without the Consent of the Congress, lay any Imposts or Duties on Imports or Exports, except what may be absolutely necessary for executing it's [sic] inspection Laws: and the net Produce of all Duties and Imposts, laid by any State on Imports or Exports, shall be for the Use of the Treasury of the United States; and all such Laws shall be subject to the Revision and Controul [sic] of the Congress" (Article I, Section 10, Clause 2).

It was the great federal preemption clause. It, along with the commerce clause, meant that whenever Congress decides that an issue involves interstate or international commerce, however tenuously, it can forbid states from regulating the enterprise. It stripped the states of their sovereign authority to maintain tariffs, import quotas, and other "barriers to trade," as they are referred to in World Trade Organization (WTO) agreements today.

"The Constitution vests in Congress plenary control over foreign and interstate commerce," wrote Charles Beard, "In a few simple words the mercantile and manufacturing interests . . . paid for their victory by large concessions to the slave-owning planters of the south."[9]

The northern framers accomplished their primary goal in jettisoning the Articles of Confederation and drafting the US Constitution. They established what today we might call the first North American Free Trade Agreement. Together with the commerce clause, which stripped state and local governments of the power to govern commercial activities that cross state boundaries, Article IV, Section 3 stripped states of authority over their prior territorial claims.[10] It gave the central government full power to add territory to the nation and expand its boundaries. It was a conscious ploy to advance the establishment of a North American economic empire without interference from We the People.

By 1825, Thomas Jefferson was alarmed enough by the federal government's use of the commerce clause to nullify the states' lawmaking authority that he wrote in a letter: "This will contain matters not intended for the public eye . . . the federal branch of our government is advancing towards the usurpation of all the rights reserved to the states. Under the power to regulate Commerce . . . and aided by a little sophistry on the words 'general welfare' a right to do, not only the acts to effect that which are specifically enumerated and permitted, but whatsoever they shall think, or pretend will be for the general welfare."[11]

That same letter went into more detail, accusing the Supreme Court, the president, and Congress of conspiring to "strip . . . the States authorities of the powers reserved by them," to favor the largest of industries over the smallest and to cut down mountains for the construction of roads and canals for private interests. Then he asked, "Are we then *to stand to our arms*?" He decided the time would be right "only when the sole alternatives left are the dissolution of our union with them, or submission to a government without limitation of powers. Between these two evils when we must make a choice, there can be no hesitation."

Commandeering oversight of commercial activities from state and local governments is justified to this day by claiming that centralized regulation serves the "general welfare." Even the most tenuous claim that a public act crosses a state border is enough to elicit claims that a national interest is involved. If it's a profitable activity or a proposed regulation that advances the project of empire, then *voilà*! It's no longer the business of the states or municipalities to oversee.

Usurpation of the majority's governing authority on this basis is, thanks to the Federalists, both constitutional and legal.

If Jefferson could have foreseen what was to become of the once plentiful forests, now clear-cut, the impoverished neighborhoods nestled in the shadow of oil refineries, and superfund sites sprinkled throughout communities like the local regulations from which big business has achieved exemption. Maybe he would say that the time for dissolving the federal union came long ago.

In 2001, the US Supreme Court ruled on a case involving a challenge by Waste Management Holdings and the owners of a landfill in Brunswick County, Virginia, against the governor of Virginia, the secretary of natural resources and the Department of Environmental Quality.[12] At issue were five state laws enacted in 1999 to limit the importation of waste from outside of Virginia for dumping in privately owned landfills.

About 30 percent of all waste disposed of in Virginia comes from out of state. A 2011 report noted that "wastes arrived in

Virginia last year from 24 states and several foreign countries, including Canada, Mexico and others in Central and South America."[13] Years before, state citizens balked at the enormous influx of trash, and state representatives responded by capping imported tonnage, banning barge shipments on several rivers, and regulating truck traffic and axle numbers.

The lawsuit against Virginia made several claims for the unconstitutionality of the state laws, but the primary charge was that they violated the US commerce clause. Congress had never ruled waste to be a commodity or a matter of commerce, but by the time of this litigation, the Supreme Court had expanded the meaning of the commerce clause so that it not only reserves to Congress exclusive power to regulate trade across borders but also "restrict[s] the powers of states to regulate or impose burdens on interstate commerce" and "in the absence of Congressional approval, [invalidates] regulatory measures designed to benefit in-state interests at the expense of out-of-state interests."[14]

Whether or not Congress had claimed a regulatory monopoly on a cross-border activity, the court held in *Fort Gratiot Sanitary Landfill, Inc. v. Michigan Department of Natural Resources* (504 US 353 [1992]) that it must be assumed it would at some time in the future, and that this option must be preserved. In *Waste Management Holdings, Inc., et al. v. Gilmore*, the court ruled against the people of Virginia and in favor of the waste-hauling industry. The court said it was unconstitutional for the commonwealth to hinder the transportation of trash into Virginia.

This interpretation of the Constitution's commerce clause is called the dormant commerce clause. With its invention, the court again fulfilled its mission to maintain and expand the Federalists' original intent to exempt the uses of wealth from public governance.

For all human history, until this ruling, what to do with waste had been a matter of local community discretion. But canny investors saw opportunity in moving urban waste out of one jurisdiction and into another. They had law on their side, and the unlucky receiving communities did not.

It's Commerce If Congress Says It Is

Every municipality, rural village, and urban metropolis is supine before the juggernaut of the Federalists' constitutional mechanisms for protecting wealth and the propertied class from obligations to community priorities. The diversity of lobbyists and industry front groups that have referred to local community lawmaking that conflicts with their business plans as a "patchwork quilt of regulations" is amusing and disturbing. The breathtaking repetition of the phrase is a reminder that wealth has a winking relationship with the law and that the appropriation of state and local authority to govern the uses of wealth is the inevitable outcome of any confrontation between community and capital.

The claim that uniformity of regulations at the state level is preferable because allowing local regulation in every municipality would make commercial ventures too burdensome disregards the interests of communities and assumes the state will represent those interests over corporate interests. But experience shows that the opposite is true. The total privatization of the public economy rests on the counterrevolutionary premise that commerce is the business of businessmen, not of the people or their elected representatives. The presumption is that the public has no legitimate role in defining or governing production, labor, and finance. Private law, including the contract clause and the commerce clause, ensures the separation of wealth and state.

Everything, whether it is privately owned fossil fuel pipe-lines, trucking, trash hauling, telecommunications, retail chains, copyrights and patents, banking, food production, medicine, alcohol, tobacco, and firearms . . . you name it . . . has been declared an issue of interstate commerce and re-moved from state and local control—that is, governance by the people. The law chooses winners based on wealth. The los-ers are derided as NIMBYs (Not in My Back Yarders).

In recent times, this ploy of invoking the commerce clause "for the general welfare" has come to include issues with doubtful relevance to interstate commerce. Here's an exam-ple that at first blush may seem a welcome invocation of the commerce clause where the general welfare was protected. Under intense political pressure "from the streets" in the 1960s, a reluctant Congress enacted laws against racial segre-gation. Lawmakers declared that they had authority to regu-late how businesses operating in multiple states treat minority customers.

In *Katzenbach v. McClung* (1964), the Supreme Court up-held Congress's authority to ban racial discrimination in res-taurants because it is a burden to interstate commerce. Instead of treating bigoted business policies as violations of constitu-tional rights, the federal government found it easier to cate-gorize racial discrimination as a regulated component of commerce. One reason for relying on the commerce clause to regulate rather than eliminate racial injustice by businesses goes back to a watershed court case that exempted wealth from public law prohibiting Bill of Rights violations.

In 1875, the Civil Rights Act was passed by Congress ban-ning racial discrimination by the hospitality, transportation, and other industries. Unhappy business owners brought a series of lawsuits against the act, claiming that Congress has no authority to regulate their treatment of customers. Eight years later, the US Supreme Court bundled and reviewed those cases in what is called the Civil Rights Cases of 1883.

To reach its conclusion, the 8–1 majority interpreted the post–Civil War Fourteenth Amendment to the Constitution in a way that had the effect of amending the amendment. As ratified, it reads, in part: "No state shall make or enforce any law which shall abridge the privileges or immunities of citizens of the United States; nor shall any state deprive any person of life, liberty, or property, without due process of law; nor deny to any person within its jurisdiction the equal protection of the laws."

All but Judge Harlan concluded that the Fourteenth Amendment forbade states from passing discriminatory laws, but that it gave no power to Congress to impose accommodating treatment of patrons on private businesses. The ruling declared businesses and corporations to be private in nature. Even though the Fourteenth Amendment prohibited states from making laws that violate "the privileges or immunities of citizens," the court determined that business entities created by state chartering and licensing laws were not "state actors," and that the state does not violate the rights of African Americans when it charters and licenses businesses that do.

As "private actors" discriminating against freed slaves, corporations and private businesses were deemed *incapable* of violating people's constitutional rights. For nearly a hundred years, the decision stood as precedent, clearing the way for Jim Crow laws and greenlighting individuals and businesses to violate minority rights at will.

According to the 1883 Civil Rights Cases ruling, it's not possible for corporate property (that is, privileged property) to be used to violate the rights of the people because it is not a "state actor." It is shielded from public responsibility because it exists in the realm of private law. The people, by contrast, through the government that ostensibly represents them, can be guilty of violating the civil rights of corporate property, which was chartered into existence in their name. The court also considered the Thirteenth Amendment and concluded that it abolished slavery but did not protect freed slaves from the "inconvenience" of discrimination by business corporations. Once again, private law immunizes privileged property from public governance. When political pressure forced the hand of the federal government to curtail racial discrimination in the 1950s and 1960s, lawmakers were reluctant to find constitutional reasons to do so. The Federalists' decedents were committed to preserving the Constitution as a guarantor of the rights *of* property, including the elite privilege of committing unfettered social indecencies. To quell increasingly violent protests, they were willing to regulate the violation of African American's basic rights as a business practice. But prohibiting private citizens and corporations from violating the unalienable rights of minorities would be inconsistent with the Federalists' original intent. Congress turned to the commerce clause as a more palatable alternative.

It was a strategy that avoided enforcing the constitutional right to equal protection of the law for everyone. Commerce clause regulation of business practices involving minorities eventually could be repealed, unlike constitutional protections. Recent assaults on and partial repeals of the Voting Rights Act of 1965, exemplify this kind of regulated (rather than unconstitutional) discrimination.

The US Supreme Court has a long history of reserving Bill of Rights constitutional protections for the corporate form of privileged property.[15] Notoriously, it has allowed Congress to regulate social injustices against people through laws couched as commercial policies. Had the justices reached a constitutional conclusion that unambiguously supported racial justice, perhaps the nation would have avoided the continuing oppression of targeted racial groups. Instead, the court and Congress legalized discrimination by "private actors" and then, when it was politically unavoidable to do so, regulated it.

Regulation: Wealth's Shock Absorber

Commerce clause "remedies" for racial discrimination set the example for environmental and labor regulation. Pigeonholing pollution and mistreatment of workers as matters of interstate commerce kept protection of the environment and the rights of workers within the realm of private law, where safeguards could be increased and decreased depending on commercial priorities.

Privatizing decisions about the rate of allowable environmental destruction and the tolerable level of mistreatment of workers on the job required Congress to create an empire of administrative agencies with authority to issue government "permits" and regulations. The permits legalize pollution, and the regulations define the *maximum* allowable protections for nature and working people. Both nature and labor are thus defined as commodities. The intended result is that the rights *of* property remain unscathed.

In historical terms, this situation is ironic. Prior to the American Revolution, John Dickinson complained bitterly of the ministerial condescension of the empire toward the colonies and how the crown put the interests of a giant corporation ahead of the rights of British subjects. He wrote that "the Rights of free States and Cities are swallowed up in Power. Subjects are considered as Property . . . Are we . . . to be given up to the disposal of the East India Company? . . . [They] would sacrifice the Lives of Thousands to preserve their Trash and enforce their measures."[16]

Following the Revolution and the Federalist counterrevolution, regulation of antisocial commercial behavior got its start. Instead of establishing outright prohibitions against assaults on community well-being, Congress and the states created a whole legal universe of administrative agencies that act as buffers between the communities harmed and the wealthy perpetrators.

The first institutional regulatory regime under the commerce clause dealt with the railroads as an interstate commercial activity. In 1887, Congress enacted legislation creating the very first federal regulatory agency, the Interstate Commerce Commission (ICC). It was sold to the public as a way to rein in the power of the railroads with rules and guidelines. Despite what was said publicly, industry leaders understood that regulation would work to their benefit. Charles F. Adams, president of the Union Pacific Railroad Company, is quoted as saying, "What is desired is something having a good sound, but quite harmless, which will impress the popular mind with the idea that a great deal is being done, when, in reality, very little is intended to be done."[17]

In 1893, then US attorney general Richard Olney assured the president of the Burlington Railroad that there was nothing for corporate bosses to worry about: "The [ICC] . . . is, or can be made, of great help to the railroads. It satisfied the popular clamor for a government supervision of the railroads, at the same time that the supervision is almost entirely nominal. Further, the older such a commission gets to be, the more inclined it will be to take the business and railroad side of things. It thus becomes a sort of barrier between the railroad corporations and the people and a sort of protection against hasty and crude legislation hostile to railroad interests."[18]

The regulatory agencies established after the ICC are no different. They have been erected as "a sort of barrier between the corporations and the people and a sort of protection against [local] legislation hostile to [corporate] interests." They protect privileged property from local democracy and against being governed directly by the people. The regulatory system has, in fact, erected a nearly impenetrable barrier between the people and their legal creations, the mighty corporations of today. And it has guaranteed that so long as citizens play along by turning to regulatory agencies for relief from corporate assaults, the privileges conferred on the propertied class will continue to go unchallenged.

Today, laws demand that people exhaust all regulatory "remedies" first, before being recognized by the courts as having grievances relative to the violation of their rights. If we are to understand how the regulatory system is used by the wealthy minority to deny the people's right of self-government, then we must be clear that regulatory law defines the parameters of what corporate officers may legally do in our communities based on minimal, not maximum or even adequate, protections for the people and environment. It then forbids municipal governments from regulating any more stringently than the state's standards. Activities that are oppressive of rights and dangerous to the community are routinely legalized with the issuance of permits. The burden of proof that harm has been inflicted rests with the victim. But it is impossible to make the case for the violation of rights within the regulatory arena. State agencies consider only whether or not a permit applicant has correctly filed official forms and supplied required information. They have no discretion to consider constitutional rights.

During the Progressive Era, historian J. Allen Smith anticipated the undemocratic outcomes to be expected from the substitution of state regulation for local self-governance, saying "Satisfactory regulation is not, as seems to be implied in much of the discussion favoring the substitution of state for local control, merely a question of placing this function in the hands of that governmental agency which has most power and prestige behind it. The power to exercise a particular function is of little consequence, unless there is an adequate guaranty that such power will be exercised in the interest of the local public for whose protection it is designed . . . [I]t should be lodged in some governmental agency directly responsible to the constituency affected."[19]

Of course, regulatory agencies are erected with no such democratic niceties in mind. An up-to-the-minute example of how this process works played out at the time of this writing. In Minnesota, a mining corporation's owners sued Winona County for enacting local legislation that banned the extraction of sand that's used in the process of fracking. Minnesota Sands' corporate directorate objected to the ban, but the Minnesota Court of Appeals found 2–1 in favor of the county.

The court ruled that because the ban affected all heavy industrial extraction and not just the sand operation, it was not a discriminatory law. Following the decision, the corporate folks issued a statement: "The ban eliminates landowner mineral rights and creates an economic risk and threat to anyone who benefits from the use of their land. We believe that allowing it to remain in place is the wrong way for Winona County to try to address issues that are beyond their authority. If Winona County has concerns related to mining within its borders, it has every right to adopt reasonable regulations instead of imposing what we continue to believe is an unconstitutional ban."[20]

The "unconstitutionality," from the corporate perspective, lay in the challenge to the corporation's Supreme Court–endowed Bill of Rights protections, along with the federal government's sole authority under the commerce clause to

regulate interstate commerce. We can anticipate that landowners and the corporate legal team will bring an appeal of
the decision, and that the outcome will reflect the corporate
statement that the residents should never have asked their
county representatives "to address issues that are beyond their
authority."

Regulation through administrative agencies is a ministerial form of governance, the very sort that American revolutionaries like Sam Adams vehemently opposed. What is
allowed and what is forbidden are determined by a central government. Communities are left to administer prescribed rules,
but not make their own. The premises on which regulation operate are predetermined by private arrangements between government and wealth. Regulatory schemes presume the legality
of harms inflicted in the course of profit making. Minnesota
Sands could claim in confidence that the county "has every
right to adopt reasonable regulations," in full knowledge that
those regulations would not block the mining, nor would they
be a burden on the company's profit seeking. Administrative
law places minimal restrictions on profitable activities that
damage communities and the environment.

Winona County's ban on sand mining may have caused the
corporate folk some inconvenience, but they were spared much
of the legal expenses for suing the county. The fees paid for
defending their interests in court are tax deductible. It's considered a reasonable cost of doing business. The county gets
no such subsidy from the government for costs involved in
protecting its citizens' rights. Nor would citizens enjoy a tax
break that would offset their costs for holding bake sales and
car washes to hire an attorney.

Bureaucratic permitting processes effectively strip states,
counties, and municipalities of the authority to govern anti-
social commercial enterprises. Everything from industrial

violations of local sanitation policies to payday lending predation has been declared a matter of private law and regulated through administrative agencies or through the courts via the commerce clause. Corporate attorneys can invoke the commerce clause as though it was just another corporate right and call on the courts to use it as a shield against local governments trying to protect community rights. The law denies that corporations can violate the people's constitutional rights, but it "knows" that local governments representing those people can violate the rights granted to corporate property by the Supreme Court.

It's no different for workers' rights than it is for the rights of communities or the environment. Labor issues are regulated as commercial activities rather than as matters of human rights. This means that laws regulating the relationship between people who work and people who profit from their work will reliably support minority profiteering at the expense of the majority who do the work. The regulations don't put businesses on notice to behave well. They put a government bureaucrat between the worker and the employer as a buffer. Letting lawmakers keep an active hand in deciding labor issues as matters of commerce ensures that the rights of working people remain negotiable and don't become constitutionalized.

In past generations, organized labor has pushed back vigorously against industrial abuse. To avoid costly disruptions of production and loss of profit, government regulatory schemes offered perfunctory concessions to workers and instituted rules of conduct. But there was never a willingness on the part of the federal courts, the states, or Congress to recognize constitutional protections for workers' rights.

Gradually it has dawned on reformers that the regulations they fought so hard to get have limited effect. Whatever protections they may think they won are subject to legal challenge. The rights of corporations and the contractual immunity from interference by government inoculate employers from having to respect the rights of workers. Over time, the regulations have been eroded and, in some cases, discarded. Because they aren't constitutionally protected rights, statutory protections *can be* eroded and discarded.

Unlike corporations, working people and the environment have nothing comparable to the commerce clause to trigger private law that works exclusively to protect their rights. When they engage in what the law calls "commercial activities," people disadvantaged for lack of privileged property are at the mercy of those owning legally fortified wealth.

Supreme Court sophistry over "private actors" and "state actors" proves the point that under US law, property rights trump human and civil rights. Simultaneous with the invention of a public sector and a private sector came the establishment of a two-track system of law. Wealth is protected as though it were an unalienable right, while unalienable rights are treated as if concessions and compromises are appropriate.

The solution to this mess is to protect unalienable rights through bedrock constitutional protections and to subject state-chartered corporations and businesses to the governing authority of the people. The US Constitution and the laws derived from it forbid this solution.

Possession Is Nine-Tenths of the Law: The Mathematics of Injustice

The northern Federalists got their commerce clause by agreeing to concessions to the southern slavocracy. Those compromises include the most startling examples of injustice to be sewn into the US Constitution. Slaves were made into a kind of privileged property. They became reservoirs of political power transferred from the people at large to plantation aristocrats. The Federalists attached powerful governing privileges to ownership of human property in the grammatically awkward three-fifths clause of the Constitution. Here it is: "Representatives and direct Taxes shall be apportioned among the several States which may be included within this Union, according to their respective Numbers, which shall be determined by adding to the whole Number of free Persons, including those bound to Service for a Term of Years, and excluding Indians not taxed, three fifths of all other Persons."

By vesting a right to political representation in enslaved human property, the Federalists knew they were indirectly elevating a host of wealthy men above all other Americans. The number of votes in the House of Representatives and the Electoral College allotted to each state was determined proportionally by population. Slaves would be counted as 60 percent of a whole human being in the census. Slave owners got an additional say in Congress and the White House by counting each natural person owing their future labor to them as 60 percent of a person.

The Federalists gave disproportionate control of the House of Representatives and the Electoral College to owners of privileged human property. That meant the southern slavocracy controlled one house of Congress, the presidency, and, indirectly, the Supreme Court.

Slaveholders' human property was more than just a source of free labor; it was a source of political power. The three-fifths clause conveyed disproportionately more governing power to a wealthy plantation aristocracy through the slaves in their possession.

In our day, private corporations are endowed with court-bestowed rights. They spend unlimited amounts on elections and legislation. Long-dead Supreme Court judges appointed by presidents chosen with the help of the three-fifths clause invented wealth-friendly legal doctrines still used today. Judicial precedent ensures the permanence of those Federalist inventions.

Wealth Turns Other People's Work into Property: The True Nature of Servitude

The last paragraph of Article IV, Section 2 in the US Constitution tells Americans that "no Person held to Service or Labour in one State, under the Laws thereof, escaping into another, shall, in Consequence of any Law or Regulation therein, be discharged from such Service or Labour, but shall be delivered up on Claim of the Party to whom such Service or Labour may be due."

To protect rights conveyed through property to slave owners and creditors, the fugitive labor clause voided these unalienable rights:

❖ The right of slaves and debtors to due process of the law. On a mere property claim, the liberty of an accused slave or debtor was forfeit.

❖ The rights of slaves and debtors to life, liberty, and the pursuit of happiness.

❖ The right of local community self-government— specifically, the right of individuals, states, local governments, and communities not to support slavery and involuntary servitude.

In 1865, the Thirteenth Amendment banned slavery and involuntary servitude. It didn't utterly gut the last paragraph of Article IV, Section 2, but only those parts specific to slavery. A creditor's claim to ownership of a debtor's future labor was deemed a legally protected form of privileged property. By not touching this aspect of the fugitive labor clause, the Thirteenth Amendment preserved rights vested in property as superior to the human and civil rights of debtors to own their own labor. One of the repercussions of that omission is that today we have a generation of people indentured through student loans, stripped of legal recourse to bankruptcy, owing a fair chunk of their productive years to people happy to receive a cut of their paychecks as pure unearned profit.

A Gentlemen's Agreement to Usurp the People's Sovereignty: Contracts *über Alles*

Chief Justice John Marshall is said to have held that in the absence of royal rule, contracts rule. The Constitution's framers evidently believed that in ridding themselves of the king, Americans had also rid themselves of a sovereign ruler. This contradicts the opinion of revolutionaries like Paine and Jefferson, who believed that with separation from the British Empire, sovereignty passed to the people as a whole.

Charles Beard noted that "none of the powers conferred by the Constitution on Congress permits a direct attack on property."[21] In fact, the Constitution methodically defines the prerogatives and privileges of wealth and prohibits government intrusion on its accumulation and use. To this end, the Federalists included the contract clause in the Constitution, which reads: "No state shall pass any law impairing the obligation of contracts" (Article I, Section 10, Clause 1).

Like that of the commerce clause, this language seems innocuous and simple to modern Americans. We are conditioned to accept it as a given that bilateral business and

financial agreements are outside the scope of general governing authority. But together the commerce and contract clauses
have the effect of elevating wealth into the pantheon of unalienable rights protected from meddling by an unsympathetic
mob.

In BOULDER COUNTY, Colorado, the city of Broomfield was
embroiled in a contest of wills and rights between a "private"
corporation, a municipal government, and the people of the
city. Local officials had signed a "memorandum of understanding" with the oil and gas corporation Sovereign, without
the consent or participation of the people. Even though they
had no part in the agreement, which would have allowed the
corporation to extract hydrocarbons within Broomfield using
the controversial process of hydraulic fracturing (fracking),
residents would be held to the terms of the contract and would
live with the resulting health and environmental damage.

In 2013, the residents exercised their right to direct democratic lawmaking. They drafted a five-year moratorium on
fracking and petitioned the measure, following existing legal
procedures, onto the ballot for a vote. The ordinance was
adopted with majority support.

Corporate attorneys claimed that the ordinance illegally
blocked them from drilling and violated its contract with the
city. According to the *Daily Camera*, "Sovereign also claims
the fracking ban violates state law, that Broomfield does not
have the authority to ban fracking, that the ban is a breach of
contract and that the company is potentially entitled to damages in the tens of millions of dollars."[22]

Local officials met with corporate representatives and
agreed to allow a judge to decide whether the local legislation
adopted by the people could block drilling from going forward.

In the end, the oil and gas industry sued to overturn the citizen-initiated ban. The court decision went against the community, nullified the law enacted by the voting majority, and cleared the way for investors to reap profits from natural gas mining in suburban neighborhoods.

The Broomfield community was initially left out of the negotiations around the "memorandum of understanding," but will have to live with the results of the contract being carried out.

Where public law reigns, policy is open to community modification through democratic processes. Where the private law of contracts controls, community priorities can be mooted by the courts. *Private* contractual business agreements aren't bound by the *public* Bill of Rights. Supposedly unalienable rights can be forfeited, confiscated, and "voluntarily" surrendered contractually. It's a clear demonstration of constitutional deference to rights vested in property and indifference to the unalienable rights of people.

Contractual arrangements are often a ploy for wealthy parties to impair the obligations of the social contract agreed to by every American who submits to the rule of law. Through nondisclosure agreements, First Amendment rights are privatized. Through out-of-court settlement agreements, the right to a jury trial is forfeited. What is lost when the jury is kept out is the people, the community, the commoners. The same goes for mandatory arbitration.

Nondisclosure agreements and intellectual property rights waivers as conditions of employment force commoners to barter their First and Fifth Amendment rights for the privilege of earning a wage. Meanwhile, the court's unchecked power to interpret the Constitution and law in consistently wealth-advantaging ways has grown exponentially. The Supreme Court retooled the contract clause in 1819 to even more intentionally destroy any remnant of local autonomy and self-government, in order to protect rights conveyed through privileged property from democracy. It's to that story that we now turn.

CHAPTER FOUR

The Emancipation of Property from Democracy

> Out of this modern civilization, economic royalists [have] carved new dynasties . . . The royalists of the economic order have conceded that political freedom was the business of the Government, but they have maintained that economic slavery was nobody's business. It was natural and perhaps human that the privileged princes of these new economic dynasties, thirsting for power, reached out for control over government itself. They created a new despotism and wrapped it in the robes of legal sanction . . . And as a result, the average man once more confronts the problem that faced the Minute Man.
>
> —Franklin D. Roosevelt

Privatizing the Village: Pulling the Rug Out from under Us

The courts have transformed the contract clause from a safeguard of bilateral business agreements into a pry bar for ripping municipal governments out of the hands of local communities.

As more of what was once considered in the public domain is given over to the so-called private sector, democratic power diminishes in proportion. More of what once was of society-wide concern is transformed into a business concern, beyond

deliberation and control by public law. This is what the enclosure and privatization of law and government look like.

The Supreme Court laid the groundwork for privatizing
local governments across the US in 1819. All it took was for
Chief Justice John Marshall and Associate Justice Joseph Story
to invent a legal distinction between "private" and "public"
corporations. Inventing this distinction, with no precedent to
rely on, made it possible to declare every municipal government in the nation the property of the state in which it is located. Doing so allowed the courts to rule that the people have
no right to use their municipal governments to make enforceable laws that serve the interests of their communities.
Marshall and Story are responsible for the legal sophistry
that tempts us to believe that local governments have no
authority to protect the people.

(The court's distinction between public and private corporations is not at all related to publicly traded versus privately
held business corporations. Both are what Marshall would cat-
egorize as private corporations in that they are chartered by
the state, and there are owners who receive the charter.)

John Marshall, a member of the Federalist Party and protégé of Alexander Hamilton, was appointed chief justice of the
US Supreme Court by John Adams at the end of his term of
office, in 1800. To deprive the succeeding president, Thomas
Jefferson, an Anti-Federalist, of a Supreme Court appointment, Adams took advantage of the Midnight Judges Act,
passed hurriedly by Congress. It authorized the reduction of
the Supreme Court from six to five members.

Justice Story was appointed to the court by President James
Madison in 1811. Also a strong Federalist, Story would tag-
team with Marshall to prove his ideological allegiance to
wealth and opposition to democracy. According to cultural
historian David Brion Davis, Story saw the pushback against

the Federalists' counterrevolution under Andrew Jackson's presidency as "oppression" of the wealthy minority's rights in property by a government representing the majority of less wealthy men.[1]

R. Kent Newmyer, professor emeritus at the University of Connecticut, and professor of law and history at the University of Connecticut School of Law, wrote that "consolidated wealth sufficient to underwrite largescale economic projects did not exist in the early nineteenth century. For the state to bestow economic prerogatives on select individuals would be to create a privileged elite which was antithetical to the principle of republican equality . . . For the state to extend corporate status, sovereign power, and economic privilege to associations of individuals, however, was a solution which satisfied both economic expediency and republican ideology. This was reflected in the phenomenal growth of business incorporation during the first three decades of the nineteenth century."[2]

Corporations chartered by the king prior to the Revolution still existed—Dartmouth College in New Hampshire, for instance. It was chartered in 1769 to serve as a kind of finishing school for the colonies' well-to-do, but also to train Native Americans to accept absorption into the European culture.

Thomas Jefferson's friend and the governor of New Hampshire, William Plumer, proposed that the school's charter be changed to make Dartmouth a state college rather than a privately run institution. The idea was to make Dartmouth the nucleus of a statewide system of public education. He went to the state legislature and asked them to draft the legislation necessary to make the change. They agreed, and soon Dartmouth became a state college with a charter that no longer enumerated the privileges once granted by the sovereign king but now placed the school under the command of the sovereign people of New Hampshire.

The trustees of the college objected. They took their case to court, claiming that the king's grant of a charter was between them and the king and none of the business of New Hampshire or its citizens. Eventually the New Hampshire Supreme Court ruled that the legislature had acted with full authority to change the terms of the corporate charter that created Dartmouth. The sovereign—that is, the people—retained their power to command the creations of their laws.

As you might guess, the trustees were not satisfied. They appealed to the federal courts, and eventually the case reached the US Supreme Court. The bizarre rulings of the court in this case set the stage for the Federalist's counterrevolution to really take off, branch out, and lay the foundation for our modern crisis of government.

The Federalists had a keen interest in the outcome of the *Dartmouth* case. They saw it as an opportunity to free the private interests of industry and capital from democratic oversight. This outcome was on Chief Justice Marshall's mind. It was on Justice Story's mind. They were looking for a legal argument that would reshape corporations as vessels of privilege for the propertied class.

Freeing corporations from the purview of public law and placing them in the realm of private law was the best course of action toward this end. But no precedent existed to justify the desired outcome. R. Kent Newmyer lays out the situation this way:

> The corporation, all agreed, was a creature of the state, "an artificial being, invisible, intangible, and existing only in contemplation of law." . . . But having been created by law, a fundamental question had to be answered: would the corporation derive its legal rights by analogy to the individuals who comprised it or from the public authority that created

it? If the former, then the corporation, in addition to the power accrued by its associative character, would fall heir to the impressive body of property rights given to individuals by Anglo-American law. If the latter, then the state could control corporate power in the interest of the public."[3]

The practical motivation for freeing private incorporated businesses from the governance of their state creators had to do with the aspirations toward commercial and continental expansion. Newmyer hints at the negative impacts on the general welfare when he writes that "to free the corporation from state regulation . . . would obscure the impact on the public of these new concentrations of political and economic power."[4]

Marshall conscripted the Constitution's contract clause to his aid, and according to Newmyer was able to conclude that "a state charter to a corporation *was also a contract* [emphasis added] within the meaning of the contract clause. The consequences of this decision were immense . . . the new business corporation came under the protective mantle of the [Constitution]. The tendency . . . to define corporate rights by reference to the authority that created them was silently abandoned. Assured of this protection, capital flowed into corporations, insuring their preeminence as vehicles of economic growth."[5]

In a concurrence that went far beyond what Marshall's arguments proposed, Story offered an expanded thesis on the new arrangement. Not only would the charter creating new business corporations become, instead of a grant of privileges from the sovereign people, a contract. Story went much further. Without precedent from American courts or the British common law, he declared that, whereas business corporations would enjoy equal status with the state that creates them, as partners in a mutual contract, "public corporations are such as exist for public political purposes only, such as towns, cities, parishes, and counties." The new municipal corporations would be state-created subunits utterly subordinate to the state and having no contractual relationship with the state.

Story saw an opportunity to magnify the status of business corporations by deflating the status of his newly defined "public" corporations used by the people to govern their local affairs. Under his novel theory, only with state permission could municipalities challenge the power of the state's contractual partners, the wealthy private corporations.

According to Newmyer, "Story understood the radical lawmaking potential of the college cause. He had followed it from its inception in New Hampshire, not as an impartial observer, but as an active partisan of the college and a useful friend of its chief counsel, Daniel Webster. Story had been one of those 'few friends' who, after the argument in 1818, had received copies of Webster's argument with instructions to 'send them to each of such Judges as you think proper.' . . . More importantly, Story advised Webster on the strategy of litigation."[6]

The Federalist judges were on a mission, and it seems they engaged in questionable ex parte communications[7] with the corporate party to the *Dartmouth* case. Their intention was clearly to shape the outcome. There was no precedent for them to follow to arrive at the novel rulings of the court. They could have ruled quite differently.

Newmyer tells us, "Conceivably, the definition of public and private might have followed function, which, in fact, Judge Richardson's decision had done [in the New Hampshire Supreme Court]. Such a functional approach to corporations would have invited American law to consider the public nature of private corporate property . . . such an analysis would have failed to put the force of law behind the creative efforts of American capitalists."[8]

By declaring business corporations to be private entities with contractual equality with the states chartering them, says Newmyer, the high court "blinded the law to certain realities of corporate power."[9]

This explains the wonder of how the Supreme Court could rule in the 1883 Civil Rights Cases that chartered businesses are "private actors," not "state actors," and thus incapable of violating constitutional rights.

So-called private business corporations (created by public chartering) became independent sovereignties with contractual agreements with the states—and by extension with the people of the states. These corporations were liberated from democratic oversight and control. "Public" municipal corporations became the property of the states, and as property they were placed in the purview of private law. The states routinely enforce severe limitations on what local governments have authority to do and, by logical extension, what citizens may do in terms of local self-government.

Because municipalities would henceforth be treated not as tools for local self-governance but as possessions of the state, the public right of self-government was privatized and removed from the public province. Where the Declaration of Independence asserted that the people are the source of governing authority, the federal Constitution, as interpreted by the court, made the states the font of governing power. The impact of this sea change was not felt immediately in the towns, cities, and boroughs of the United States.

In the early nineteenth century, municipalities had few conflicts with the interests of capital and property. Later, when industrialization directly impacted the interests and rights of municipal residents, the contest between public and private corporations became more frequent, until today litigation over whether rights in property or rights in people will prevail is a daily occurrence.

To review, Marshall's court imposed two big changes in the realm of corporations. First, because a municipal corporation would now be a state-owned administrative unit rather than a community government through which the democratic rights of residents could be expressed, it would have no legal agency commensurate with the autonomy of private business corporations.

Second, the charter given to private business corporations would no longer represent privileges bestowed on the incorporators by the sovereign people. Going forward, the so-called private charter would be a contract between the state issuing the charter in the name of the people and the individuals receiving it. The incorporators would have legal agency to govern the corporation independent of state control.

It is important to note that because the charter was now a contract, the state could not unilaterally alter the internal affairs of the business corporation or revoke its self-governing authority. The same cannot be said for public municipal corporations or the rights of unbanked citizens to govern themselves.

To understand the implications of this two-part judicial revolution is to know the story of how the Federalists achieved a stupendous victory for wealth over commoners. The judiciary yoked the general population in every state to a central government doling out privileges for the rich, and disenfranchising all of us from democratic control of our local communities. Compounding this intolerable situation, business corporations have been armed to the teeth by law to invade municipal jurisdictions and exploit communities across the continent, backed by the US Constitution's commerce clause and the contract clause, since the *Dartmouth* counter-revolution.

Managers of for-profit business corporations, especially those engaged in interstate commerce, are in a superior position that allows them to treat municipalities as resource colonies. Nominal regulation legalizes their harmful extractive and monopolistic practices while lending a veneer of protective limitations on the damage they can inflict. The distinction the Federalists made between corporate privileged property and public state-owned municipal corporations not only emancipated the rich from democracy but gave them a powerful tool with which to govern our communities in our place.

A Second-Class Township and Its Second-Class Citizens

The commonwealth of Pennsylvania classifies its municipalities as cities, boroughs, and townships, and further categorizes them by class, based on population. By far the most numerous type of municipality is what's known as a "township of the second class." According to the Pennsylvania State Association of Township Supervisors (PSATS), townships account for 95 percent of the commonwealth's land area and are home to 44 percent of its population. There are more than fourteen hundred townships of the second class. It should be no surprise that the people living in them are treated like second-class citizens.

That's how the folks in Grant Township, Pennsylvania, felt when a judge told them they have no authority to protect themselves against dangerous toxins that a corporation called Pennsylvania General Energy (PGE) planned to inject into the ground under their homes.

In 2014, the people of Grant got wind of a spin-off money-saving project related to fracking, the extraction of natural gas by a process involving pumping a secret concoction of toxic chemicals deep into underground rock formations to crack them open and release the combustible vapors. When millions of gallons of the protected trade-secret potion are pumped down under extreme pressure, what's loosened gets forced up and out. That includes methane and other fossil fuels, but also highly saturated brine, radioactive minerals and gases, and the toxins used to shatter the rock formation.

The flow-back waste material is collected above ground. Disposing of it used to mean trucking it to Ohio, where the rules for pumping it back into the ground under high pressure were laxer than in Pennsylvania. The cost of transporting the waste out of state cut into the profits of the mining company; eventually, however, industry lobbyists won the day, and the Pennsylvania state legislature loosened its rules. The company eyed little Grant Township, home to fewer than eight hundred people, as the site for only the third injection well in the state.

The families living in Grant depend on well water to survive. They had heard about how the people of Dimmock, Pennsylvania, and other towns in the commonwealth had their clear, clean drinking water turned into a dark-brown smelly brew because of fracking. They didn't want that to happen in their township, so they enlisted CELDF's Pennsylvania community rights organizer, Chad Nicholson, who worked with the local community group—the East Run Hellbenders Society (named after a giant local salamander)—to draft a law that would elevate the rights of the community above corporate property and ban frack waste disposal within the municipality.

In the summer of 2014, the township advertised the ordinance in advance of voting on its passage. The board of su-

pervisors soon received a letter from the corporation's attorney
threatening litigation that would ask the court for damages
and legal costs if the ordinance was enacted.

The threat didn't stop adoption of a Community Bill of
Rights that recognized the right of the people of Grant Township to clean air and water and a right of local community
self-government to protect those rights. It also included a
provision that CELDF has championed since 2006: it recognized legally enforceable rights for ecosystems.

It was a defensive piece of legislation. The ordinance said
it would be a violation of the people's and nature's rights for
the company to site an injection well in the community.

PGE corporation hit Grant Township with a lawsuit that
said the municipal corporation was violating the business corporation's civil rights. It also said the municipality had no
legal authorization from the state to enact such a ban. It was
a claim with roots in John Marshall and Joseph Story's creative invention of private corporations for the wealthy and
public corporations for commoners. The people had no controlling interest in the municipal corporation, as the owners
and directors of PGE did in theirs.

When the lawsuit came, the municipal officials sent their
legal representatives from CELDF to argue for the residents'
right to protect their water, health, and environment with a
local ban on the industrial threat. Then, in October 2015, magistrate judge Susan Baxter ruled on the case without consid-
ering those arguments.

She overturned the parts of the ordinance that prohibited
depositing oil and gas mining waste in the municipality and
that subordinated so-called corporate rights to the unalienable rights of community residents. The rationalization for a
judicial veto of these parts of the township's law was this:
Under Pennsylvania law, Grant Township was a township of

the second class, governed not by the people living in the municipality but by a municipal code written by the state legislature and subject to absolute state control.

The ruling said that the municipal government, which the people had elected to represent them, has no legal authority to make or enforce governing decisions to protect the community without state permission. At best they could administer nominal state regulations but could not prohibit what the state had permitted.

The underlying message was that when the state issues permits to legalize the use of privileged property cloaked in the trappings of a private corporation, the people may protest, but they can't prohibit the profitable violation of the community's rights.

Grant Township is what community organizers call a "sacrifice zone." That's a place where wealth's privileges legally usurp the rights of the people who live there. What's sacrificed is health, safety, and environmental sustainability, along with the democratic rights of the people. They are given over to the rights vested in property enjoyed by the owners of a wealthy corporation, with the complicity of a state that claims to own and control Grant Township and every other municipality within its borders.

When the people of Grant Township and their municipal board of supervisors received Judge Baxter's decision, they weren't surprised. Not only were they expecting it, but they had planned for it. Even before the court stripped their community rights ordinance down to its bare bones, the Hellbenders and their allies organized a campaign to change Grant from the official status of a township of the second class to a home rule municipality.

Going home rule would require electing what in Pennsylvania is called a Government Study Commission made up of seven community members. When elected, those seven would constitute a kind of local constitutional convention, charged with writing a home rule charter, the legal equivalent of a local constitution. They intended to write and adopt a local constitution rooted in unalienable rights.

Even before the court rejected their local ordinance in October, as the Hellbenders and the Grant supervisors anticipated it would, they elected their Study Commission at the primary election in May of that year. Then, in November, less than two months after the judge's decision, the Study Commission proposed a charter that was placed on the ballot and adopted overwhelmingly by a vote of the people of Grant.

Grant's legal counsel, CELDF, applied to the court for dismissal of all complaints pertaining to the ordinance since the local law had been made moot with adoption of the home rule charter. The court declined to act on this filing. Judge Baxter's decision to protect the rights of the corporation against the municipality's "unconstitutional" ordinance was accompanied by notice of a jury trial to determine what damages and legal fees Grant would have to pay to PGE to make the corporation whole again.

Then the state went on the attack. With the judiciary busily representing the interests of PGE, an executive branch agency filed suit against the township. It became a national story when the Pennsylvania Department of Environmental Protection (DEP) sued Grant Township for protecting its environment more thoroughly than state law allows. "Ceiling preemption" raised its head. The suit argued that the ordinance illegally held DEP personnel liable for violating the community's rights when they issued permits to a corporation, thereby legalizing the injection of poisons into the ground.

During the PGE litigation, a temporary settlement was reached with the agency when Grant agreed not to enforce that single provision of the ordinance that put DEP employees in legal jeopardy.

Piling on, Judge Baxter agreed with a request by the PGE industrialists to sanction the CELDF attorneys who had argued the case for Grant Township. Baxter imposed monetary sanctions against the attorneys in the amount of $52,000. One of the attorneys was also referred to a disciplinary board of the Pennsylvania Bar Association.

What lawyerly misbehavior was being sanctioned? Judge Baxter said the attorneys had repeatedly sought to vindicate the community's right of local self-government despite the court's repeated refusal to recognize it as a valid right. The judge also found it intolerable that the attorneys had repeatedly argued that the legal rights bestowed on corporations could not be used to defeat the rights of the residents of the municipality. Baxter claimed that such arguments were "frivolous" and sanctionable. She agreed with the PGE legal team that the CELDF lawyers should be fined and, if possible, disbarred for proposing such audacious legal theories.

Her sanctions against CELDF attorneys are currently pending appeal.

The legal doctrine that made it possible for the court to overturn the original Community Bill of Rights and then nullify parts of Grant Township's home rule constitution was a spin-off of the Supreme Court's *Dartmouth* ruling. It was grounded in a legal theory based on *Dartmouth* that ignores the democratic rights of the residents of municipalities and champions the autonomous powers lodged in business corporations. The doctrine was developed after the Civil War to free a burgeoning industrial economy from the constraints of local law.

It is called "Dillon's Rule."

CHAPTER FIVE

The Municipal Colonies of America

Let the National Government be entrusted with the defense of the nation and its foreign and federal relations; the State governments with the civil rights, laws, police and adminis-tration of what concerns the State generally; the counties with the local concerns of the counties, and each ward direct the interests within itself . . . It is by dividing and subdividing these republics from the great national one down through all its subordinations, until it ends in the administration of every man's farm by himself; by placing under everyone what his own eye may superintend, that all will be done for the best.
—Thomas Jefferson

Dillon's Rule and John Marshall's Dead Hand

There was a respite from constitutional meddling in local gov-ernments by the court during the early nineteenth century while the expanding American empire claimed more and more of the North American commons for itself. It created new territories and states. As it grew, new communities were intentionally established as municipal corporations. Towns long established prior to the states and the nation jealously guarded their autonomous status and rejected incorporation. But as empire rolled out across the continent on the iron bars of the railroad corporations, judges stepped in to defend the conquest and turn communities into colonies of the states.

There were early expectations in America, following the Revolution, that community life would be guided locally, democratically, by community decision-making. The traditional New England town meeting perhaps came closest to the ideal. There, every eligible elector had a say in the regular business of the community. But it was not only in Massachusetts, Rhode Island, New Hampshire, and Connecticut that the ideal of direct citizen participation shaped local government.

The Township Act of 1798 in New Jersey incorporated 104 communities under a direct-democracy town meeting style of government. White males twenty-one years of age and older who were residents of the town for six months, paid taxes, owned land, or paid rent of at least $5 per year were eligible to vote. Direct limited democracy in the townships was retained until 1899, when major revisions to the Township Act abolished the town meeting, and a township committee assumed municipal legislative powers.[1]

Public opposition to establishing towns as municipal corporations was particularly keen in Boston, where town meetings embodied the ideal of communities making their own governing decisions with broad participation.

> Thus one pamphleteer lauded the existing town-meeting structure as "the greatest and most precious Privilege any Town or Society can be possessed of" while direly predicting that "the Rich will exert the Right of Dominion" in a government of aldermen and councilors. With the advent of the municipal corporation . . . "the Great Men will no more have the Dissatisfaction of seeing their Poorer Neighbors stand up for equal Privileges with them in the highest Acts of Town Government." Instead, under corporate rule these

"Great Men' will gain control, and Rich & Poor Men then will no more be jumbled together in Town Offices."[2]

Opposition by Federalists to direct citizen legislation was strong. James Madison, a critic of town meetings, wrote in *Federalist* No. 55, "In all very numerous assemblies, of whatever characters composed, passion never fails to wrest the scepter from reason. Had every Athenian citizen been a Socrates, every Athenian assembly would still have been a mob."

Thus the so-called founding fathers of aristocratic temperament refused to accept that the American Revolution had finally established community self-determination. As we've seen, it was with the 1819 *Dartmouth v. Woodward* ruling that the court took the first step in freeing business corporations from governance by the people. The decision was eventually to prove fatal to the exercise of self-governing rights in American communities.

Following *Dartmouth*, popular consternation was reflected in loud protests and even the burning of Judge Marshall in effigy because his court emancipated business corporations from democratic governance. But at first no one noticed Judge Story's contribution to the decision, which shackled local governments to the will of the states in which they are located. According to Hendrik Hartog, chair of the History of American Law and Liberty Program at Princeton, that's because "the law of municipal corporations had not been invented."[3] In the first few decades following the *Dartmouth* ruling, the courts rarely ruled on the nature and scope of local government authority. Later in the century, when business corporations had grown in power and began to compete with local governments for control of resources and rights-of-way, things changed.

Explaining further, Hartog has written,

> One reason why there was no "law" of municipal corpora-
> tions was because chartered cities were already part of an
> undifferentiated "law" of corporations. Indeed, in the 1820s
> treatise writers still considered the borough the paradigm of
> corporation existence, echoing the traditional common law
> perception of a corporation as *"property investing the people
> of a place with its local government"* [emphasis added] . . .
> For Stewart Kyd, whose *Treatise on the Law of Corporations*
> remained the leading work on both sides of the Atlantic
> until the 1830s; boroughs were simply one type of civil cor-
> poration. Nothing distinguished public from private entities;
> those terms played no part in his analysis."[4]

Despite the *Dartmouth* ruling, the right of the people to
use municipal corporations to engage in local democratic self-
government was not challenged with ferocity until the end of
the Civil War. American courts and legislatures declined to
make a distinction between so-called private and public corporations, despite the *Dartmouth* ruling, until incorporated
municipalities became the vehicles for an expanded suffrage
to influence the allocation of resources and the regulation of
businesses. Once the uses of municipal corporations expanded
beyond the protection of property interests, they no longer
served the agenda of latter-day Federalists.

That transition marked a change in the deference shown
to municipal autonomy by state governments. So long as governance of the locality was used to protect property, the state
took a *laissez faire* stance. However, once the private nature of
the charter waned and the city, borough, or town began to behave in the public sphere, representing nonproperty interests
of the inhabitants, state deference was withdrawn.

The state withdrew chartered governing rights on the presumption that the municipal corporation and the people it spoke for should not be allowed to make judgments impacting private ownership rights unless the municipality was made directly answerable to the state legislature. In this way, the role of the legislature as representative of property privileges and not of unalienable rights was further clarified.

The *Dartmouth* decision was dusted off and reinvigorated in 1868 by the railroad lawyer turned Iowa Supreme Court judge, John Forest Dillon. Dillon spelled out what *Dartmouth* had tentatively accomplished for the propertied class. In *City of Clinton v. Cedar Rapids and Missouri River Rail Road Company,* he revived the court's privilege-affirming and rights-denying dicta with a ruling that protected a railroad corporation from a community's local lawmaking.

Following Judge Story's lead, Dillon denied the community's authority to use the municipal corporation to enact laws to protect community interests against the business plans of the Missouri River Rail Road Company. He summarized his opinion years later in a legal treatise saying, "the great weight of authority denies *in toto* the existence, in the absence of special constitutional provisions, of any inherent right of local self-government which is beyond legislative control."[5]

The shorthand Dillon used to summarize this opinion goes like this: Local government is to the state as a child is to a parent—a dependent entity that has no legal agency of its own.

Modern legalese is a bit less direct. *Duhaime's Law Dictionary* defines Dillon's Rule this way: "A rule of judicial interpretation that a municipality may exercise only those powers expressly conferred by statute, necessarily or fairly implied by the expressed power in the statute, or essential and not merely convenient."

Dillon's Rule isn't in the US Constitution. It's a legal opinion that aggressively implements the antidemocratic potential of the *Dartmouth* ruling. Dillon went even further than Judge Story. Not only did he think states' ownership of municipal corporations gave the states authority to alter or abolish any powers delegated to the municipality; he extended the power of the state to deny "in toto" the right of the people to local self-government.

This is important. Dillon asserted that the people's right of local self-government had been vested, with the adoption of the federal constitution, in municipal property owned by the states. It's an argument that purported to turn the right of local self-governance into a right vested in property owned by the state. By vesting what had been the democratic rights of the people in municipal property owned by the state, Dillon privatized, enclosed, and cut off from public governance the unalienable right of self-governance.

Here we have another example of the court making the rights *of* property publicly enforceable while privatizing the right of self-government.

As a form of property infused with once-public rights, municipal corporations became privileged property. Municipal corporations convey to the state the right to govern the "tenants," as Dillon called the people dwelling within the jurisdiction of a municipality. The people and their democratic rights were thus subordinated to property, as the Federalists intended.

Dartmouth by way of the contract clause stripped every American of the right of local self-governance. Inspired by *Dartmouth*, Dillon's Rule, like the contract clause, is a form of private law enforced as public law. And like other private laws, it is exempt from public alteration, regulation, or revocation.

If the states own the municipal corporations, then who owns the states? If not the people, then who? Why is it a question of ownership, anyway? The answer is to be found in the system of government that the Federalists erected. In every legal confrontation between unalienable rights and the rights vested in property, the courts never fail to remember the will of their dead Federalist masters. Dillon remembered Marshall, and judges today remember Dillon. As a result, all municipal subdivisions of the states have been privatized, their governance centralized in the state, where the controlling interests of an aristocracy of wealth hold sway.

Revolutions have been justified for lesser transgressions of the public trust. If the Federalists could betray so fair and just a revolution as was waged with Tom Paine's inspiration, then the majority is supine and has no place to retreat. If we are to take a stand, it must be in the communities where we live. That has been the strategy of CELDF's community rights organizers since 2002.

Resource Colonies, Not Hometowns: The Legal Status of Municipalities

The right to govern every American community is up for grabs by whatever combination of wealth takes control of the state legislatures. It's true that Congress can be relied on to forbid municipal and state governments from enacting laws to assert the will of the governed community, through the commerce clause. That requires lobbying and campaign funding at the national level. But the states are the more regular culprits when it comes to inventing pretexts for stripping citizens of local governing rights. Lawmakers do it by revoking all meaningful authority from the municipal corporations the people would otherwise use for this purpose.

There have been hundreds of recent state enactments focused on subordinating the rights of communities to the prerogatives of the propertied class. Just a few examples will do.

In 2005, the Pennsylvania state legislature enacted the ACRE initiative as Act 38, at the urging of agribusiness and waste-hauling lobbyists, including the PA Farm Bureau and PennAg, a consortium of factory-farm corporations. This law empowers the citizen-elected state attorney general to sue municipalities to overturn local laws that regulate or ban factory farms and urban sludge dumping.

Notably, Act 38 places the highest law enforcement officer of the state at the private disposal of corporate waste and agribusiness interests. The legislators "representing" these communities enacted this measure after scores of municipalities adopted local rights-based ordinances to protect their residents and natural environment. CELDF organizers were instrumental in working with those communities, and in lobbying against an even more draconian version of the bill. Similar aggressive laws against community self-government continue to be adopted by state legislatures across the nation and around the world.

Less than a decade later, with widespread local opposition to the process of fracking, industry "nonprofit" advocacy groups busily lobbied dozens of state legislatures to enact preemptions that would block local fracking bans, prohibitions on pipelines, and bans on export terminals and other industrial infrastructure. In Texas, soon after the city of Denton banned fracking by popular demand, the legislature passed a ban on such local bans.

Texas House Bill 2595 followed directly on the heels of the ban on local frack bans. It prohibits cities from validating initiative petitions for local ordinances that would "restrict the right of any **person** to use or access private property for economic gain. That means if voters in a city attempted to petition to, for example, ban hydraulic fracking, as they did in Denton, the petition would be tossed out [before the first signature was gathered] because it violates the rights [*sic*] of mineral owners."[6]

THESE AND THEIR MANY companion preemptions are the legacy of the *Dartmouth* ruling. Everything from local bans on plastic shopping bags, to minimum wages, to prohibitions on water privatization and assault weapons have been overturned at the request of corporate lawyers and front groups. The denial of community self-governing rights is encoded in a legal theory that, like the terms *corporation* and *political party,* cannot be found in the US Constitution.

The cynicism of proponents of Dillon's Rule and of the planned incapacity of every American to engage in self-government at home is boundless. While agreeing that each citizen has a constitutional and natural right of self-government, they argue that the state has the authority to forbid public corporations—municipal state property—from being used for the purpose.

It is akin to the state conceding that the law guarantees the right of every citizen to ride a horse, and then enacting a law that prohibits any horse from bearing a rider.

Business Corporations Are For-Profit; Municipalities Are for Profit

Judge Story's category of public municipal corporations includes not just general-purpose governing municipalities—

such as cites, boroughs, towns, and so forth—but also development corporations, water authorities, and school districts. Certain types, especially development corporations, are regularly chartered at the request of commercial interests, so that it is a wealthy minority, empowered by public rights and money vested in state property, who directly benefit.

The creation of new towns, boroughs, and cities became a municipal marathon during the nineteenth century, as the territorial claims of the American continental empire expanded westward. University of Michigan research professor Nancy Burns tells us that the idea of erecting new communities through incorporation had no legal merit except as it advanced the speculative and pecuniary designs of land "developers." She writes, "The first general incorporation law passed in the Louisiana Territory in 1808. Nine years later, similar legislation passed in Indiana and Ohio. In 1825, Missouri passed a general incorporation law. Nine states soon followed."

Burns continues:

> One example of the efforts of these early developers is the founding of Grand Junction, Colorado. In 1881, settlers were officially allowed into western Colorado. To ensure that the town they wished to build would have citizens, the speculators pressed settlers to incorporate the town of Grand Junction. The thirty-three voters complied. The speculators set up all the ingredients of the town; they built the post office, started a newspaper, imported residents, and set up the meeting to propose incorporation. The developers paid the first mayor's way to the federal land office in Leadville to file for incorporation. As [Kenneth T.] Jackson and [Stanley K.] Shultz argue, in nineteenth century America, real-estate speculators spent much of their time building cities.[7]

The rules for municipal annexation and for incorporating a municipality out of unincorporated land in a county or township vary from state to state, but regularly give the largest landowners the authority to allow or disallow changes in governing jurisdictions. Local majorities are left out of the decision-making. In short, it is the interests of property and wealth that can partake of "local self-government" in a way that is even more effective than early property qualifications at keeping the rabble—that is, community majorities—out of the business of governing and defining new governments.

Anti-Dillon: It Didn't Have to Be This Way

To the continued chagrin of the friends of democracy, the legal establishment, at the same time that it embraced John Forrest Dillon's legal theory, rejected the opinion of Michigan Supreme Court judge Thomas Cooley, one of the era's leading scholars of constitutional law. Cooley argued that municipalities receive their power directly from the people and thus have a kind of limited autonomy. It is the state's power to curtail local authority that is limited—by general rights.

Cooley wrote in 1871 that "the sovereign people had delegated only part of their sovereignty to the states. They preserved the remainder for themselves in written and unwritten constitutional limitations on governmental actions. One important limitation was the people's right to local self-government."[8]

Cooley argued that for the people to create state legislatures and then subordinate themselves to their dictates would be absurd. It would contradict the principles espoused in the Declaration of Independence, which says that "to secure these rights, governments are instituted among men, deriving their just powers from the consent of the governed."

But through a long chain of decisions, the courts have generally rejected Cooley. Dillon's Rule was not a legally necessary conclusion. It was a choice made by judges to side with property against general rights.

Officials elected to merely administer state law within local jurisdictions cower in the shadow of Dillon's Rule. Using the single most often heard excuse for why they cannot or will not enact protective measures when requested by residents of the municipality, they regularly inform their local constituents that they "wish they could help, but their hands are tied."

During a weekend Democracy School, I presented the municipal structure of local governance to members of the Lakota nation residing at Pine Ridge Reservation in South Dakota. A class participant gazed at an illustration I'd drawn on a flip chart. After some silent contemplation, she announced: "Huh, the white man's municipalities are just reservations, like ours. The difference is, we know we live on reservations. The white man doesn't."

That about sums it up.

Local Self-Government and the American Revolution

What was really on the minds of average American colonists when they revolted against the empire is easy to discover. Their complaints are listed in the Declaration of Independence. Let's take a quick look at the Declaration and compare the vision of self-government it laid out to the government we ended up with. Did it really call for a central government with veto power over every American community's laws? Did it demand that democratic rights either serve commerce and wealth or face the usurping preemption of Congress, the Supreme Court, and every state?

The Declaration signed on July 4th, 1776, wasn't the original work of Thomas Jefferson, although he gets most of the credit. Some of the inspiring language was lifted from the writings and speeches of the Levellers and Diggers of England. A century before the American Revolution, those radical groups had manned the New Model Army that Oliver Cromwell and the wealthy men of commerce raised to depose King Charles I.

Jefferson borrowed such phrases as "consent of the governed" and such ideas as "the people are the source of governing authority" from the peasants who demanded that the British House of Commons be revamped to represent the common people, and that, everyone being equal, peasants should take the reins of power in England.

When Jefferson listed the colonist's grievances against the Crown, he borrowed from resolutions sent to the Continental Congress by more than ninety towns and counties throughout the colonies.[9] Among the thirty or so complaints he listed, the very first one mentioned in Jefferson's Declaration is the preemption of local laws by the central government: "HE [the king] has refused his Assent to Laws, the most wholesome and necessary for the public Good."

The revolutionaries were not talking about being prevented from making state or federal laws. There were no "states," and there was no nation. It was the usurpation of the people's right to enact and enforce laws in their own communities that had them up in arms.

Today, across the country, this is exactly what is happening in town after town.[10] States and the federal government are preempting local laws intended to protect workers, immigrants, and the homeless, and to fend off resource stripping, toxin dumping, and property confiscation.[11] What American revolutionaries listed as their first order of business to correct through revolution is now the chief counterrevolutionary proj-ect of such organizations as the American Legislative Exchange Council. Today's Federalists are as opposed to democracy as were their predecessors.

This first salvo against the empire's preemption of local laws was not the last. Other complaints filled the second half of the Declaration. Most of them condemned interference from London in matters of local self-government. In the ab-sence of local lawmaking authority, appointed colonial gov-ernors were also forbidden to enact laws that represented colonial interests. The Declaration says, "HE has forbidden his Governors to pass Laws of immediate and pressing Impor-tance, unless suspended in their Operation till his Assent should be obtained; and when so suspended, he has utterly ne-glected to attend to them."

In many states today, local laws have no effect until they are approved by officers of the state.

The revolutionaries rejected the paternalistic idea that the empire would wisely provide for colonial needs so long as the colonists abandoned their right to representation in Parlia-ment. On this point the Declaration says, "HE has refused to pass other Laws for the Accommodation of large Districts of People, unless those People would relinquish the Right of Representation in the Legislature, a Right inestimable to them, and formidable to Tyrants only."

We're no better off today. The Federalist's frame of govern-ment that replaced British rule institutionalized the exile of American communities from legislative representation. How-ever well state voting districts are drawn, even without bla-tantly partisan gerrymandering, communities per se have no representation in state legislatures, as we'll see in chapter 7.

Americans today have a lot in common with the colonists who found their lives and freedoms curtailed by bureaucratic shell games. The next grievance Jefferson listed against the empire read, "HE has called together Legislative Bodies at Places unusual, uncomfortable, and distant from the Depository of their public Records, for the sole Purpose of fatiguing them into Compliance with his Measures."

What activist hasn't had to skip a day of work and travel to a hearing halfway across the state to testify before legislators, bureaucrats, and regulators? It's a situation that would be rare if the people's representatives remained in the communities they supposedly serve, to learn the will of their constituents, rather than gather in ostentatious capitols where lobbyists and paid persuaders have their ear every day.

Like municipal residents across America today, the revolutionaries were outraged when the empire legalized the violation of people's rights. And when colonists challenged that oppression with local laws to protect their safety, the empire nullified, vetoed, and preempted them, rendering local officials and local laws irrelevant. Jefferson framed their complaint this way: "HE has dissolved Representative Houses repeatedly, for opposing with manly Firmness his Invasions on the Rights of the People."

Modern regulatory agencies have multiplied into an alphabet soup of administrative bodies. By the time American colonists decided to declare their independence, a similar bureaucracy, referred to as a *ministerial* form of government, had been imposed on the colonies. The Declaration documents the colonists' grievance. "HE has erected a Multitude of new Offices and sent hither Swarms of Officers to harass our People and eat out their Substance."

This "ministerial" style of government places bureaucrats between the 99 percent and the propertied 1 percent who have the real authority to make decisions. Anyone who has ever had their hopes of prevailing at a regulatory hearing dashed

because the agency lacked discretionary power will understand how the colonists felt.

These days, Americans can find their local attempts at
democratic legislation preempted by international trade agreements. Treaties that protect foreign business interests against
local laws that "erect barriers to free trade" were no stranger
to the revolutionaries. They objected to such imperial policies
that ignored their right of self-determination, and Jefferson included that objection in the Declaration: "HE has combined
with others to subject us to a Jurisdiction foreign to our Constitution, and unacknowledged by our Laws; giving his Assent
to their Acts of pretended Legislation."

American courts today don't consider the Declaration of Independence a precedent-setting document. That makes sense
only when we realize that the Federalist counterrevolution
opposed its democratizing doctrines. Robert L. Brunhouse
wrote a detailed account of how unpropertied commoners took
control of the Pennsylvania colonial assembly in 1776 and
precipitated a vote in the Continental Congress to adopt the
Declaration.[12] Without their insurrection against property
qualifications for voting and holding office, New York and other
states would not have agreed to the Declaration, and the colonies would not have seceded from the British Empire.

Brunhouse's book documents how, following adoption of
an ultrademocratic state constitution in Pennsylvania and the
Revolution's success by commoners in pursuit of parallel aspirations, the Federalists' counterrevolution unraveled those
democratic gains with their conspiratorial drafting and rush
to ratify their federal constitution.

The government the Federalists gave us mimics the one
that justified the Declaration of Independence. Reviewing the
"causes which impel[led] them to the separation" from England
puts into perspective our plight today. It can help us under-

stand why people in a growing number of American communities are challenging their treatment as mere colonies of the empire.

Federalist False Flag Waving: Irony and the Star-Spangled Banner

The federalism we got is not what American revolutionaries fought for. The missing ingredient under the current system of government is people deciding their own affairs.

Reference to local government cannot be found in the US Constitution. Latter-day Federalists justify this oversight claiming that efficiency demands that local governments comply with state and federal micromanagement. Anti-Federalist Thomas Jefferson and his mostly rural colleagues disagreed. While the urban Federalist minority spread disinformation as they pressed for a new constitution, Anti-Federalists protested vehemently. The lead-up to ratification of the Constitution saw threats of tarring and feathering, among other coercive scare tactics, for anyone who openly opposed its ratification.

Americans today uncritically accept the Federalists' betrayal as the intended realization of our nation's revolutionary heritage. We need to shake free of this deception. We can't correct the mistakes of the past without admitting them and without rejecting the legal obligation to repeat them as hallowed precedent in every legal proceeding.

Average Americans believe that the Federalists were the founding fathers. They celebrate them on national holidays with bunting and stars and stripes everywhere. But they celebrate a changeling history. False memory has replaced truth with fact-free flag-waving. Even the old yarn about Betsy Ross and the stars and stripes covers up the irony of the Federalists' true loyalties.

The American flag is a close replica of the banner flown by the British East India Company,[13] the giant British corporation whose tea Sam Adams and the Sons of Liberty dumped into Boston Harbor. Those hotheads were protesting the treatment of American colonists as second-class British citizens. They thought Americans deserved representation in the British Parliament and that the company's directors, who engineered a corporate tax amnesty, didn't deserve better treatment than colonists who had to make up for the empire's lost revenue through a tax on tea.

As is the case today, it was the owners of chartered corporations, not unbanked and underbanked people, who held sway over government. Now those corporate red and white stripes are flown triumphantly across the continent. Curious minds might wonder who really won the Revolutionary War.

CHAPTER SIX

The New Three-Fifths Clause

> *Civil government, so far as it is instituted for the security of property, is in reality instituted for the defence of the rich against the poor, or of those who have some property against those who have none at all.*
>
> —Adam Smith

Two Hundred Years of Chartered Injustice: Evidently You *Can* Make This Stuff Up

Historians have called the American Civil War the "second American revolution," the "bourgeois revolution," and the "corporate revolution." By whatever rubric, its end marked a watershed moment in the ascending fortunes of wealth toward the pinnacle of power. Huge tracts of federal land were transferred from public ownership into the private possession of corporate investors, thanks to the war debt owed by the federal government to the railroads, arms and textile manufacturers, coal barons, and especially the banks. Political paybacks also transformed the federal judiciary and the US Senate. They were suddenly bursting with corporate lawyers after the war. Under that new proprietorship, the Supreme Court exercised astonishing boldness when it unexpectedly "discovered" corporations in the Constitution—where they are never mentioned.

The 1886 *Santa Clara County v. Southern Pacific Railroad Company* ruling declared, without precedent or argument, that corporations are to be treated as "persons" and afforded protection of the law equal to any human being. That opened the door for more than a century of legal victories for the propertied class that culminated with the infamous *Citizens United* and *Hobby Lobby*[1] decisions.

Once the door was open, the robed men and women of the court, with nothing but the force of their opinions, amended the Constitution and transformed the nation from a nominal republic into a de facto plutocracy.

In 1866, Congress approved the Fourteenth Amendment and sent it to the states for ratification. In 1868, three quarters of the states did just that. Then in 1886, the Supreme Court amended the amendment, using the *Santa Clara County* case as cover to declare that where the Fourteenth Amendment says, "nor shall any State deprive any **person** of life, liberty, or property, without due process of law; nor deny to any **person** within its jurisdiction the equal protection of the laws," the word "person" applies to chartered corporations too. That meant that beginning on May 10, 1886, and forever after, it would be unconstitutional for any state to deny corporate property the same legal protections given to people.

Let's unpack that a bit. Recall that sixty-seven years earlier, the Supreme Court decided in the *Dartmouth* case that a charter of incorporation would no longer be a grant of certain commercial privileges from the whole of the people to a few members of society desiring to establish a business corporation. After February 2, 1819, every charter became a legal contract between the people of the state and the people receiving the charter. The *Dartmouth* decision declared that after the charter was publicly issued, it immediately became a matter of private law, and it would be unconstitutional under the contract clause for a state to "impair the obligation" of the contract.

When in 1886 the court declared that corporations are persons deserving the protection of the Fourteenth Amendment's equal protection clause, the "contracts" between the people and the incorporators of every corporation in every state were altered. The court's *Santa Clara* decision contractually obligated the people of the states issuing corporate charters to conditions they had never agreed to.

Without discussion, the court declared that contracts in the form of corporate charters would now bind the people issuing the charter to recognize their corporate creations as persons with unalienable rights. The states were simultaneously preempted by the contract clause from "impairing" court-mandated terms of the contractual charter and from making laws that deny corporations the same legal protections as citizens.

After the fact, the people were excluded from governing their corporate creations because contracts are within the province of private law.

Chief Justice Morrison R. Waite presided over the *Santa Clara* case. The dispute was over taxes and whether Santa Clara County, California, could tax the Southern Pacific Railroad at a higher rate than the county taxed people. The court said that such taxation would violate the corporation's right to equal protection of the law. It would, in fact, be unconstitutional discrimination and a violation of the corporation's civil rights. Our history demonstrates that the court has been reluctant to exhibit anywhere near this level of homage to the rights of flesh-and-blood persons.

There is some irony in the fact that Judge Waite had also presided over a case in 1874 in which Virginia Happersett of Missouri argued that as a citizen of the United States, she had an equal right to vote, protected by the new Fourteenth Amendment. Waite replied to Ms. Happersett that "Our province is to decide what the law is, not to declare what it should be," and dismissed her claim.

In 1896, the court further amended the Fourteenth Amendment when it decided that although it had been ratified to guarantee equal protection of the law to freed slaves, states could constitutionally segregate African Americans from white Americans. With the *Plessy v. Ferguson* decision, racial discrimination became constitutional on May 18, 1896, ten years after the court made it unconstitutional to discriminate against corporate property. Not until May 17, 1954, was this irrational and bigoted decision overturned in *Brown v. Board of Education of Topeka.*

Since 1886 it has been unconstitutional for the states that charter corporations to discriminate against them. Meanwhile, the struggles of flesh-and-blood persons for racial and gender equality, for democratic rights, for protection against corporate assaults continue, with institutional opposition from government. The privileges of the propertied class are shielded from governance by the people through preemption, the privacy of contracts, ceiling regulations, federal hegemony over interstate commerce, and the privatization of government by dissembling judicial decisions backed up by the coercive power of public law. That's the law the people supposedly govern with.

Corporations Are Not the Problem: The Diversion of "Personhood"

Corporate "personhood" has gotten a lot of attention since the Supreme Court's *Citizens United* ruling. The 2010 case built on decisions made by politically appointed judges over nearly two centuries. It expanded the ways that corporate property can convey to its owners both enhanced political clout and immunity from public censure.

But let's be clear. Corporations don't spend money on elections. The truth is that specific people use corporate property as conduits through which they spend large quantities of money to control the outcome of elections. They are privileged with power over and above the rest of us because they are not held to account for their actions. They are above the law, thanks to the privileged property they possess and the shield of corporate immunity from liability.

Only a fanciful suspension of reality could enable the Supreme Court to conclude that the First Amendment is applied equally when corporate managers are allowed to control political discourse by purchasing it in the name of the corporate "person" they own. Talk of corporate personhood diverts us from noticing that it is wealthy human beings, not property itself, who received the privilege to decide who will govern from the court.

The Federalists did their worst to violate the ideals of the Revolution when they vested the right of representation within the chattel property of slaves via the three-fifths clause. When the Thirteenth Amendment overturned not only slavery but the three-fifths clause along with it, the imperious Supreme Court was quick to replace the propertied elite's lost political advantages. The antebellum Constitution that had lodged extra congressional and electoral college representation for plantation plutocrats in their chattel property was put back on track when the court vested political rights in corporate property.

Where the slave once played the role of privileged property, the corporation now fills the bill. In effect, vesting rights in property denies the constitutional right to a republican form of government and creates political advantages for a favored wealthy few.

Today, because the Supreme Court vested rights in corporate property and granted the propertied class the power to fund campaigns through their corporations, all elective positions of power are available for purchase by the wealthy investor class. It's a better deal for the 1 percent than the plantation owners got.

According to James F. Epperson, "in the 1950s, only 2% of American families owned corporation stocks equal in value to the 1860 value of a single slave. Thus, slave ownership was much more widespread in the South than corporate investment was in 1950s America."[2] Today, stock in corporations is more broadly distributed than in the 1950s, but control of corporations and how they spend money ("speak") to influence election outcomes is not. According to Rob Wile of *Money* magazine, "The top 10% of American households, as defined by total wealth, now own 84% of all stocks in 2016, according to a recent paper by NYU economist Edward N. Wolff."[3]

Prior to 1865, the slave was not responsible for depriving white men in the north of their right to equal representation in the federal government. The men who crafted the Constitution's three-fifths clause were responsible, and the political imbalance they created resulted in the Civil War.

Twenty-one years after the end of that national fratricide, corporate lawyers presiding on the Supreme Court engaged in mutation through interpretation of the Fourteenth Amendment and filled the void left by revocation of the three-fifths clause. Those ideologically driven men are responsible for the resulting violation of public political rights that now exceed the damage done by the three-fifths clause. And every political appointee to the court who has added to the rights vested in corporate property over the ensuing years is responsible for the deep societal stress now in evidence, brought on by the cumulative injustice of privatizing general rights.

Whether or not the Federalists foresaw the potential for turning charters of incorporation into instruments for empowering the propertied class and disempowering the rabble, it is certain that their revolutionary nemesis, Thomas Paine, understood the tyrannical nature of chartered privileges. He and revolutionaries such as Sam Adams knew firsthand how the commercial aristocracy had used charters as weapons of oppression prior to the Revolution. The revolutionary Sons of Liberty distributed numerous broadsides against the corrupting influence of the great corporations of the era. The true revolutionaries, not the Federalists, understood that exclusive privileges and monopolies were ruinous to general rights.

Paine had no illusions about the purpose of corporate charters. He explained in simple terms that they are legal tools that create advantages for a privileged few at the expense of everyone else. Paine was ridiculed mercilessly in the British press for writing that human rights are an inherent birthright superior to inheritable aristocratic privileges. He didn't rise to the bait of brutal political cartoons caricaturing him as "Mad Tom." Instead, he went straight to the root of the problem, writing, "I answer not to falsehood or abuse, but proceed to the defects of the English Government. I begin with charters and corporations."

Then he dove in, saying, "It is a perversion of terms to say that a charter gives rights. It operates by a contrary effect— that of taking rights away. Rights are inherently in all the inhabitants; but charters, by annulling those rights, in the majority, leave the right, by exclusion, in the hands of a few . . . Those whose rights are guaranteed, by not being taken away, exercise no other rights than as members of the community they are entitled to without a charter . . . therefore, all charters . . . are instruments of injustice."[4]

The US Constitution, seen as a charter, operates in the same way through its commerce and contract clauses, and through every word of judicial dicta that transformed public rights into privatized rights under the private law of corporate charters and contracts. The Supreme Court has perpetuated and enhanced those privatized rights from one generation to the next. The propertied class, not corporations, deprives the rest of us of our right to a representative form of government through the powers stored in their privileged property. Property itself, including corporations, does not bear the burden of responsibility.

After witnessing the passage of the first four presidential administrations, Thomas Jefferson seemed to sense the disastrous detour away from the ideals of the Revolution that America had taken. In 1816, the year the *Dartmouth* controversy went to court, he wrote that "England exhibits . . . an example of the truth of the maxim that . . . ruin will fall heaviest, as it ought to fall, on that hereditary aristocracy which has for generations been preparing the catastrophe. I hope we shall take warning from the example and crush in its birth the aristocracy of our monied corporations which dare already to challenge our government to a trial of strength, and to bid defiance to the laws of their country."[5]

Jefferson saw the equivalence between the British hereditary aristocracy and the "aristocracy of our monied corporations." He predicted that it would all end badly for the people, and that the coming catastrophe would be a direct result of allowing a privileged minority to act beyond the governing authority of the community at large.

A year later, even the author of the Constitution's first draft, James Madison, was having second thoughts. He wrote, "there is an evil which ought to be guarded against in the indefinite accumulation of property from the capacity of holding it in perpetuity by corporations. The power of all corporations ought to be limited in this respect. The growing wealth acquired by them never fails to be a source of abuses."[6]

That was over two hundred years ago. Since then, the power of corporations has burgeoned.

The Contract on America: The Constitution as Forced Arbitration

The federal court has illegitimately contractually obligated the people of every state to involuntarily honor the rights the court vested in corporate property. I won't recount the many high court decisions that have without precedent handed most of the Bill of Rights to the propertied class by vesting them in the fictitious personhood of corporate property. For a timeline of those disastrous decisions, see CELDF's *Model Legal Brief for the Elimination of Corporate "Rights,"*[7] Adam Winkler's *We the Corporations: How American Businesses Won Their Civil Rights* (2018), and Thom Hartmann's *Unequal Protection: How Corporations Became "People"—And How You Can Fight Back* (2002).

The enhanced Bill of Rights immunities from public law that the Supreme Court judges transmitted to the propertied class through their corporate property include the following:

❖ Legal protection of wealth equal to the unalienable rights of people

❖ Procedural and substantive due process of law for wealth involved in legal disputes

❖ Immunity of wealth from public governance

❖ Amplification of the right of free speech for the wealthy above the volume of public discourse when they use corporate property as the conduit for their opinions

❖ Money redefined as "speech," freeing up the propertied class to purchase elections and legislation

❖ Freedom for the corporate class to assert religious dogma as a political weapon

❖ Freedom from warrantless search and seizure, including unscheduled OSHA, EPA, and other inspections to guarantee compliance with public regulations

❖ Freedom from double jeopardy regardless of judicial error or postacquittal discovery of guilt

❖ Freedom from government "takings of property," including permits and licenses, hypothetical "future profits," and access to "resources," regardless of harms caused to people and the environment

❖ Liberty of privacy, including the right not to disclose ingredients of foods or components of toxic industrial materials, or to produce papers and correspondences that would reveal incriminating evidence of malfeasance, lawbreaking, and perjury

❖ Freedom to face an accuser in a court of law and deduct legal expenses as a cost of doing business

To say that the modern business corporation is the preeminent form of privileged property today is an understatement.

The question arises, did those judges honestly interpret the Constitution when they determined that corporate property is a person deserving the same rights as people? Or were they dishonest in their rulings and simply granting privileges to the rich indirectly by bestowing their privileged property with immunity from public governance?

The 1886 *Santa Clara* case that created a precedent for corporations being treated as legal persons opened with Chief Justice Waite declaring, prior to oral argument, that "the court does not wish to hear argument on the question whether the provision in the Fourteenth Amendment to the Constitution, which forbids a State to deny to any person within its jurisdiction the equal protection of the laws, applies to these corporations. We are all of the opinion that it does."

A persuasive argument has been made that the Southern Pacific Railroad's legal representative in the case, Roscoe Conkling, who at the time was the last living member of the drafting committee for the Fourteenth Amendment, deceived the court into believing that the intent of the committee had been to include corporations under the meaning of the word "person" in the amendment.[8] The details of the controversy are beyond the scope of this book. But the court clearly departed from reliance on precedent in coming to its unsupported conclusion.

Years later (in 1938), Supreme Court justice Hugo Black wrote, "in 1886, this Court in the case of *Santa Clara County v. Southern Pacific Railroad*, decided for the first time that the word 'person' in the amendment did in some instances include corporations . . . The history of the amendment proves that the people were told that its purpose was to protect weak and helpless human beings and were not told that it was intended to remove corporations in any fashion from the control of state governments . . . The language of the amendment itself does not support the theory that it was passed for the benefit of corporations."[9]

Supreme Court judges are obligated to execute the program laid out in the US Constitution and in the "case law" of prior court decisions. When it came time to invent a place for corporate property in the Bill of Rights, the court ignored the lack of precedent and went to the spirit of the Constitution, where they found deference to rights in property supplanting rights in people as a matter of course. Following *Santa Clara,* the court regularly pointed to it as precedent even though Justice Waite's declaration that corporations are persons was no part of the ruling in the case. We live with the fallout every day.

Rights Vested in Property Privatize Civil Rights

As soon as an employee parks the car in the lot outside and enters through the door to the workplace, she leaves her civil rights in the glove compartment. Settling in to her cubicle, she notices an email from the personnel department. She is informed that the online search she did during her lunch break the previous day is a violation of company policy and an unauthorized use of corporate property for personal business. A note of reprimand will be entered in her file. Her right of privacy has not been violated, because the corporation that employs her is, according to case law, not a "state actor" and is not capable of violating her rights, even though it was created by a state-issued charter and licensed to do business by the state.

Across town at another state-chartered organization, a warehouse worker is pulled aside and instructed to report to the office for a random drug test. His employment is on the line if he refuses. His Fourth Amendment right against warrantless search has not been violated, according to court precedent. The corporation is not considered a "state actor" by the judiciary.

Across the continent in a factory that molds plastic into bumpers for the auto industry, a worker on the line nods to a coworker and says, "maybe we need a union." Minutes later she is standing in front of the vice president's desk being told that there will be no talk of unions on the job.

According to the courts, her First Amendment right of free speech has not been violated for the same reason the rights of the other employees were not. Only the state, and not "private actors," can violate rights. Wealthy people in possession of "private" business corporations own privileged property that is chartered by a state government. They were made immune from responsibility for violating rights. The law says they are not capable of infringing on the rights of employees.

A week later, this employee is required to attend a special meeting where management presents its arguments against workers unionizing. It is a mandatory meeting. And no, her First Amendment right of free association has not been violated. Even the National Labor Relations Board, the regulatory agency that mediates disputes between employees and employers, informs her a few days later that she has no case for a civil rights violation. The corporation has a First Amendment right to lobby employees on the job to oppose collective bargaining. Workers have no right, while on corporate property, to campaign for unionization.

Another right the employees don't have on the job is the right to participate in corporate business decisions. The people who will make the products and produce the added value to raw materials have no say in what will be produced or whether the raw materials will be extracted with environmental, community, and worker safety in mind. They will not be consulted about hazardous materials that will become part of the product or be used in its manufacture.

Once chartered, the corporation becomes a sovereign entity independent of the state that made it. The chartering state and the sovereign people of that state have no say in the corporation's internal governance. This is how private law subordinates the unalienable rights of people, and public law has no authority to check the abuses of private power. Those abuses are legalized by ownership of privileged property. The human beings pulling the strings behind the corporate curtain are protected from liability by the rights *of* property.

It is difficult to understand the acquiescence of so many of us to all of this.

Property's War against You and Me: The Constitution Deputizes the Corporation

The US Constitution allows Congress to "declare War, grant Letters of Marque and Reprisal, and make Rules concerning Captures on Land and Water" (Article I, Section 8, Clause 11). At the same time, it forbids the states from granting letters of marque (Article I, Section 10, Clause 1). Owing to the federal court's insertion of Bill of Rights protections into state-issued corporate charters, those supposed contracts with the state have taken the place of letters of marque, which once were issued to "privateers" in time of war, authorizing them to attack enemies of the empire.

The British Empire used chartered corporations such as the East India Company (which once had a standing army larger than England's), the Hudson Bay Company, and others to colonize once independent communities around the globe. Those corporate charters purported to license the companies to invade, overturn local governments, extract resources, and coerce free/cheap labor from the conquered people. The corporate charters of modern business juggernauts today function the same way.

Powered by extraordinary legal rights vested in property, the trend is leading us away from public governance of society and toward private dominion over everything. Schools, hospitals, highways, and prisons are all being privatized. Public land is auctioned off for exploitation with no benefit to the public. Water supplies are taken over by for-profit enterprises. Mercenary armed forces are paid with public monies. In the crosshairs for annihilation since they were first established are Social Security, Medicare, and other New Deal/Great Society programs.

James B. Weaver was twice elected to the US House of Representatives and twice a candidate for the presidency. In 1892, he wrote that "the creation of corporations for pecuniary profit . . . bears strong resemblance to the practice among Nations of granting letters of marque, except that there is never any preceding offense to justify it."[10]

Are the American people enemies of the empire? Perhaps because the Federalists' plan of government was framed in hostility to commoners, this is the inexorable outcome at a time when the empire's global reach is contracting. When exploitation of foreign resources is slowed, an inward turn and the cannibalization of domestic resources, both human and natural, become inevitable. Exempted from obedience to local laws, corporate privateers now treat municipalities like resource colonies. Property's empire bloats temporarily as it devours its own.

Like the charter of the British Empire's East India Company against which American revolutionaries rebelled, court-ordered constitutional privileges for chartered incorporations of property have empowered privateering minorities shielded by corporate immunity to raid and acquire resources for themselves and helped grow property's empire. Today's privateers raid foreign and domestic communities with impunity to gather their resources in an undeclared war of continued conquest against these communities.

Still, we are wrong to blame corporations. They are the weapons, not the perpetrators. The true menace, and what must be exposed to a so-far credulous population, is the privileged minority that sees humanity and life itself as resources for their enrichment.

Pushing Back: The People Say "Not So Fast"

In 2002, after discussing the way corporate lawyers stop municipalities from blocking factory farms and urban sludge dumping by threatening the local government with lawsuits for violating the corporations' "civil rights," Mic Robertson, a local official in Licking Township, Clarion County, asked CELDF's cofounder Thomas Linzey to write a law that would deny that corporations are "persons" with the same rights as people. Thomas did. And it became township law.

Mic's simple question laid the groundwork for CELDF to include limitations and outright nullifications of corporate "rights" in every local law we've drafted since then. Here's an excerpt from a second CELDF ordinance adopted by Licking Township in 2010:

> Rights of Licking Township residents secured by this Ordinance and by other local, state, or federal law, shall not be subordinated to the claimed rights, which are in-fact privileges, of state-chartered corporations. Accordingly, public and private corporations that violate the prohibitions of this Ordinance shall not enjoy privileges or powers under the law that make community majorities subordinate to them or have the effect of nullifying this Ordinance. Nor shall corporations possess the authority to enforce State or federal preemptive laws against the people of Licking Township that would have the effect of nullifying this Ordinance. Within Licking Township, corporations shall not be "persons" under the United States or Pennsylvania Constitutions, or under the

laws of the United States, Pennsylvania, Licking Township, or any other law, and so shall not have the rights of persons under those constitutions and laws.

It wasn't naiveté, and it wasn't hubris that led us to challenge existing law. We didn't pretend to have overturned the Supreme Court's rulings over the past century. What we began to do in 2002 and continue to do today is educate and inspire people to act on the premise that their unalienable rights are the highest law and the justification for government, as the Declaration of Independence makes clear. We knew that before we could challenge and defeat the Federalists' counterrevolution, we would have to end their occupation of the American mind. That meant doing things "everybody knows" we couldn't do.

CHAPTER SEVEN

The Pretense of Representation

To the shock and dismay of land-based elites, the workers who poured into the cities between 1870 and 1920 challenged elite rule through Democratic Party machines and the Socialist Party. So the growth elites created a "good government" ideology and a set of "reforms" that literally changed the nature of local governments and took them out of the reach of the upstarts.

—William G. Domhoff

One Step Forward, Two Steps Back

During colonial times and up until the mid-1840s, the right to vote and hold public office in many states could be exercised only by white men who owned a minimum amount of property. The poor white man's civil rights movement was one of the first people's movements to wrest exclusive authority to govern from the hands of the land-owning gentry, or so they thought.

Judicial maneuvers like the *Dartmouth* decision allowed the propertied class to strip municipalities of autonomous governing authority and thereby minimize the political gains won by propertyless white men. Historian J. Allen Smith described how this new impediment to local lawmaking arose within a generation of the final extension of the rights of suffrage to white men without land:

> It is easily seen that the removal of property qualifications for voting and office-holding has had the effect of retarding the movement toward universal municipal home rule. Before universal suffrage was established the property-owning class was in control of both state and city government. This made state interference in local affairs unnecessary for the protection of property. But with the introduction of universal suffrage the conservative element which dominated the state government naturally favored a policy of state interference as the only means of protecting the property-owning class in the cities. In this they were actively supported by the corrupt politicians and selfish business interests that sought to exploit the cities for private ends. Our municipal conditions are thus the natural result of this alliance between conservatism and corruption.[1]

It was the expansion of voting rights to white men who were not property holders that prompted federal and state leaders to retract the authority of local governments to legislate and enforce local laws. Allowing a larger, predominantly unbanked and underbanked electorate to make local laws that reined in the power of money was unacceptable to the ruling class. Smith said of the times,

> The attitude of the well-to-do classes toward local self-government was profoundly influenced by the extension of the suffrage ... the removal of property qualifications tended to divest the old ruling class of its control in local affairs. Thereafter, property owners regarded with distrust

local government, in which they were outnumbered by the newly enfranchised voters. The fact that they may have believed in a large measure of local self-government when there were suitable restrictions on the right to vote and to hold public office, did not prevent them from advocating an increase in state control after the adoption of manhood suffrage.[2]

When voting rights were extended to black males with the Fifteenth Amendment and eventually to women with the Nineteenth Amendment, the propertied class focused more purposefully on disenfranchising them from meaningful local self-government.

Dillon's Rule, which resurrected the *Dartmouth* decision on municipal subordination to states, was intoned from the Iowa bench in 1868. In 1870, the Fifteenth Amendment guaranteed the right of suffrage to all men regardless of "race, color, or previous condition of servitude." In 1891, with European immigration in high gear, the US Supreme Court made Dillon's Rule apply to every municipality in the nation, and the court doubled down, making Dillon's Rule the law of the land in 1907. The effect on local democracy was profoundly negative.

According to Alan Trachtenberg, professor emeritus of English and American studies at Yale University, during the period of rapid industrialization, corporate-controlled policymakers supported an unparalleled influx of immigrants. With a rash of farmstead divestiture, relocation of the dispossessed to the cities and the influx of newcomers from abroad made for larger municipal communities. These developments alarmed those same policymakers. Their top priority became minimizing what effect extending the right to vote to a rapidly expanding unbanked and underbanked population would have at the local level.

New arrivals in the Northeast taking jobs in the coalfields, factories, and rail yards transformed American politics, according to Trachtenberg, as surely as did the emancipation of the slaves in the South. Expectant immigrants arrived with aspirations for democratic participation and found that they were the least welcome of Americans except in as much as their bodies could become prosthetics for the corporate class's will to power.[3]

The political parties pandered to ethnic interests and perfected a machine politics that played on social divisions. Federalist descendants—of both major parties—strove to remove representation of municipal communities in state legislatures. Where *Dartmouth* and Dillon's Rule stripped municipalities of their authority to govern on behalf of local populations, representation of counties and municipalities in state legislatures was disrupted with the invention of politically drawn voting districts. By atomizing individual voters into districts that were blind to municipal and community cohesion, the political parties, which are private corporations run by the wealthy class, made collective political action by the hoi polloi impossible.

Residents of American municipalities became statistics that could be manipulated and lumped into consciously structured assemblages that served the priorities of the two-party cartel representing the rights *of* property. The people's right of association as communities was desecrated so that the collective might of the people could not turn democracy against the whims of wealth.

Grouping voters in legislative districts based on party affiliation took the power of the franchise out of the hands of citizens and put it under the control of the propertied class. Private political parties gained a new weapon to fend off democratic collaboration among citizens. They had in effect invented a new form of privileged property: the ballots of commoners alienated from their communities and packaged into predictably compliant voting blocs.

The practice came to be called *gerrymandering* after Elbridge Gerry, one of the Massachusetts delegates to the 1787 Philadelphia Federalist convention. He is one of the delegates who refused to sign the US Constitution for lack of a Bill of Rights, but he then served as the country's fifth vice president under James Madison. Gerry once wrote, "Democracy is the worst . . . of all political evils."[4]

In 1887, one writer for organized labor noted that "the members of the [state] legislature were not chosen, as at present, by divisions of counties, but were elected by the county on what we would call a general ticket—so that they represented not a mere number of individuals, but the counties or groups of associated individuals. Not till 1846 were the supervisors authorized, in this State, to divide counties into election districts."[5]

And so, in the same year that Thomas Dorr's Rhode Island rebellion finalized the nationwide civil rights struggle for "universal white manhood suffrage," the political party system representing institutionalized wealth inaugurated its strategy to shrink the power of each of those new votes.

Diminishing Returns on Democracy

European immigration to the United States was integral to the transformation of American communities into colonies of property's empire. According to environmental, social, and political historian Samuel P. Hays, between 1820 and 1860 approximately five million people entered the country. Between 1860 and 1890, thirteen-and-a-half million came, and between 1900 and 1930, almost nineteen million crossed the Atlantic, for a total of thirty-seven-and-a-half million people between 1820 and 1930.

By 1900, recent immigrants accounted for about 40 percent of the residents in the twelve largest American cities, with another 20 percent being second-generation immigrants.[6] Loyalty to the party was cultivated as a surrogate for lost community cohesion. Local party bosses took to instituting systems of patronage, nepotism, and favor-trading.

Reformist middle-class progressives, seeing their political clout in American society being challenged by a large influx of immigrants and what they saw as the corruption of the political parties, devised programs for professionalizing urban and municipal government. Their schemes mirrored the internal governance of the giant corporations. Efficiency, not democracy, became their watchword. They believed that well-educated, financially successful men, not the sordid majority, should govern American communities.

The planned dysfunction of municipal government, much like today's planned dysfunction of public schools, created an excuse for reformers to advance plans to privatize many municipal functions. Progressives offered new templates for local government modeled on corporate management.

Ethnic neighborhoods resisted such "reforms." Despite majority resistance, progressive efforts to put a sheen of respectability on local government resulted in high-sounding reforms that in the end had the effect of subtracting the people from local government.

Among the progressive's democratizing proposals, and there were factions that put them forward with integrity, was the creation of "home rule" municipalities. The idea was for "public" municipal corporations to be freed from state dictates. To do this, local constitutions, or home rule charters, were tendered. They would allow citizen initiative, referendum, and recall, meaning that residents of the community could propose new laws, oppose ones enacted by the local government, and remove unresponsive representatives from office through a petitioning process and vote. In some (mostly western) states, the powers of municipal initiative, referendum, and recall were ratified as state constitutional amendments.

Although municipal home rule was being peddled as a tool for progressive reform, the reformers by and large did not intend to craft home rule as a vehicle for handing over the authority to govern local affairs to peasant majorities. Martin Schiesl, professor emeritus of history at California State University, Los Angeles, says this about the urban progressives: "Like other middle-class groups who interpreted democracy in terms of property rights and assumed that government should be in the hands of the well-educated and 'respectable' people, they were frightened by the growing social and political influence of immigrants and workers. They therefore denounced the party system which permitted the lower class people to acquire such power."[7]

In "The Failure of Universal Suffrage" Francis Parkman wrote, "Two enemies, unknown before, have risen like spirits of darkness on our social and political horizon—an ignorant proletariat and a half-taught plutocracy."[8]

Parkman called for a crusade against democracy itself.[9]

Martin Schiesl illuminates this sentiment further: "To reform-minded members of the middle-class who had a deep and abiding respect for a political system that . . . usually protected the wealth and position of its most 'valuable' citizens, it appeared that popular government had broken out of the stable framework in which smaller communities had contained it. Now, to their eyes, mass democracy ran reckless through the large cities and threatened not only private property but also the authority of local institutions."[10]

According to Schiesl, historian Francis Parkman believed that the "diseases of the body politic gathered to a head in the cities and it was there that the need of attacking them was most urgent." It was "indiscriminate suffrage" that allowed an "ignorant proletariat" to gain political power.

When the Nineteenth Amendment secured the right of women to vote in 1920, even nominal municipal reform and especially the drive for local initiative and referendum rights began to run out of steam. Two world wars intervened, and the right of local community self-government languished, a victim of American power projected beyond the borders of all our municipalities.

There Is a Right of Communities to Govern Themselves Called Freedom

The right of the people to local community self-government continues to be suffocated by the special privileges protected in American law as the rights *of* property and the privileges those rights convey to the wealthy. The result is that democracy is subordinated to those special privileges. Through tradition, precedent, case law, and a false system of justice, the fate of every American is tied to whatever an opulent propertied class contrives to accomplish. All because the Federalists refused to trust the people, believing they knew better than anyone what all of us want and need.

The current conservative campaign for voter suppression, hostility toward immigrants, and the disenfranchising effects of mass incarceration continue the drive to privatize control over who will vote and who will not, and whether the votes that are cast can have any effect on policy and power.

The courts deny that collective community rights exist, as reflected in the near eradication of class action suits and the aggressive judicial defense of Dillon's Rule. Collectivization of rights prevails only insofar as corporations are argued to be voluntary associations of people rather than legal entities with rights of their own.[11]

That collectivist right to exercise self-government is permitted within "private" corporations only because the sole legal purpose of such a corporation is profitable accumulation, privatization, and the creation of property. It's the brick-laying of empire.

Local Community Self-Government in Action Today

To ensure that their rights would continue to stand even against preemptions by legislatures and precedent-addicted judges, dozens of communities have included citizen enforcement provisions in their local laws. One example was enacted by Plymouth, New Hampshire, on January 25, 2018. The project threatening the community's rights is known as the Northern Pass, a large, unsustainable "energy corridor" that industrialists want to route from Canada across the state.

Part of the people's declaration regarding the proposal stated that "We the people of Plymouth declare that unsustainable energy projects violate the rights of Plymouth residents, including our right to make decisions about what happens to the places where we live. We the people of Plymouth find that certain commercial energy projects are economically and environmentally unsustainable, in that they damage property values and ecosystems, place the health of residents at risk, threaten the quality of natural systems within the Town, while failing to provide real benefits to the people of this community."

The town warrant went on: "We the people of Plymouth find the current environmental laws allow state-chartered corporations to inflict damage on local ecosystems that cannot be reversed, violating the rights of residents to protect their community and the rights of ecosystems to exist."

And then there is the citizen enforcement section: "The Town of Plymouth, or any natural person domiciled in Plymouth, may enforce all of the provisions of this law through an action brought in any court possessing jurisdiction over activities occurring within Plymouth. In such an action, the Town of Plymouth or the natural person shall be entitled to recover all costs of litigation, including, without limitation, expert and attorney's fees."

OTHER COMMUNITIES HAVE TAKEN a further step, embracing their rights as the highest law. The Lafayette, Colorado, Climate Bill of Rights and Protections ordinance, adopted March 17, 2017, included this statement: "All residents of the City of Lafayette possess the right to a form of governance which recognizes that all power is inherent in the people of the City, and that all free governments are founded on the people's authority and consent. Laws adopted by the people of the City shall only be preempted or nullified if they interfere with rights secured by the state or federal constitution to the people of the City, or if they interfere with protections provided to the people or ecosystems of the City by state, federal, or international law."

Thanks to the good work of CELDF organizer Chad Nicholson, Grant Township, of which much has been written, was one of the earliest communities to legalize nonviolent direct action in defense of community rights. Here's that part of their home rule ordinance, enacted in May 2016. Under the heading "Right to Directly Enforce People's Rights," it says this: "If a court fails to uphold the Grant Township home rule charter's limitations on corporate power, or otherwise fails to uphold the rights secured by Article I of the charter, the rights and prohibitions secured by the charter shall not be affected by that judicial failure, and any natural person may then enforce the rights and prohibitions of the charter through direct action. If enforcement through nonviolent direct action is commenced, this law shall prohibit any private or public actor from bringing criminal charges or filing any civil or other criminal action against those participating in nonviolent direct action."

It is no mystery why American courts will find this statement as illegitimate and unenforceable as the assertion in the Declaration of Independence that "to secure these [unalienable] Rights, Governments are instituted among Men, deriving their just Powers from the Consent of the Governed, that whenever any Form of Government becomes destructive of these Ends, it is the Right of the People to alter or to abolish it." Justification for the American Revolution was premised on wholly different values than those held by the Federalists who wrote the counterrevolutionary property-and-commerce Constitution. The judges who channel those long-dead Federalists are no friends of democracy. Of course not. That's not their job.

Because the interests of local communities involve the preservation and protection of rights other than the rights *of* property, they have been divorced from the Federalists' frame of government. We the People will remain in exile so long as we do not take a stand for our legitimate rights, chief among them the right to govern collectively with our neighbors in our communities. Self-government is up to us, not political parties and their handpicked minions. Democracy is trickle-up, not trickle-down.

CHAPTER EIGHT

Creditors and Cannibals

Poverty is that state and condition in society where the individual has no surplus labour in store, or, in other words, no property or means of subsistence but what is derived from the constant exercise of industry in the various occupations of life. Poverty is therefore a most necessary and indispensable ingredient in society, without which nations and communities could not exist in a state of civilization. It is the lot of man. It is the source of wealth, since without poverty, there could be no labour; there could be no riches, no refinement, no comfort, and no benefit to those who may be possessed of wealth.
—Patrick Colquhoun

No Property, No Rights

Debt is a claim of ownership by the wealthy of the productive capacity of other people. Today it's a claim with global reach, thanks to neoliberal policies. The world has seen the muscles and brains of paupers harnessed to the will of an opulent minority for the building of empire.

In North America, a wealthy aristocracy fueled by stolen labor went well beyond constitutionalized slavery, and embraced Alexander Hamilton's notion of a profit-making, self-perpetuating engine for economic growth fueled by debt. Creating profit from debt is no more novel than the idea of planned scarcity driving up prices and hence profits. A scarcity of money is as effective as a scarcity of food or water in compelling unbanked and underbanked people to sell their labor at a cut rate. What is needed today and can't wait for tomorrow can be bought on credit, the collateral being an excessive obligation to perform future work in payment.

The origin of Hamilton's dominion-making machine goes back to the privatization of the commons in England, where land never owned by anyone was privatized by legal fiat, fenced, and titled with legal deeds. This era of confiscation of public assets for transfer into private ownership raised a small minority of privileged men high above the rest. The people dispossessed of their traditional homes were given the option of staying on the land as serfs who would "owe" a significant portion of their crops and labor to the lord who now owned the manor. This "debt" was an artificial creation of the law, a kind of antiproperty that illustrates how granting property privileges to some can only be sustained by taking freedom from servitude from the rest.

In England, the propertied class enacted a whole set of laws collectively known as "the terrors," which, among other things, criminalized vagabonds who refused to stay in servitude on privatized land. The crime of being "landless and masterless" was punishable by imprisonment and torture. Mercantilists could legally kidnap vagrants and force them into indentured servitude in the "new world" colonies that were similarly stolen from indigenous people and privatized.

Linebaugh and Rediker state, "In England the expropriation of the peasantry was accomplished by systematic violence and terror, organized through the criminal sanction, public searches, the prisons, martial law, capital punishment, banishment, forced labor, and colonization."[1]

Today the criminalization and enslavement of people in poverty are better camouflaged but no less oppressive. Victimless "criminals" are said to owe a debt to society. The labor of predominantly African American prisoners is rented out to corporate masters while their civil rights, including the right to vote, are suspended.

Debt is the new face of enslavement. No clearer current example presents itself than the so-called student loan debt crisis. Wealthy lenders now legally own the future labor of a whole generation, and those debtor scholars have no means of escape from debt slavery—because the law favors rights in property over rights in people. Usury—high interest rates for the least privileged—creates wealth for the creditor, who is indenturing the future labor of the debtor and suspending the right of freedom from servitude.

The Rap on Alexander Hamilton

The Broadway musical *Hamilton* has given this Federalist counterrevolutionary misappropriated legitimacy as one of America's founding heroes. The misinformation about Hamilton has been amplified by lionizing him in rap and rhapsody.

Alexander Hamilton, unlike Thomas Paine, is remembered in marble and bronze in the nation's capital. And his face is on the $10 bill. First secretary of the treasury under the second Constitution, he tagged along with Washington throughout the Revolution. He also followed the general's lead when it came to cheating commoners out of what little they owned. He got so good at it that he made it the basis for enriching and empowering the new federal government and the class of men who forged it. It wasn't an arbitrary choice; he was preparing the new nation for continental expansion, hemispheric colonialism, and eventual global empire.

Hamilton's grand idea was to make debt the cornerstone on which to build that empire by leveraging it into a tool for spending borrowed money today, for private gain, and indenturing people without wealth to fund the Ponzi scheme with their future labor. The debt-indentured commoners never contracted to be parties to the arrangement, nor did their children and grandchildren.

Payments on this generalized debt are collected as taxes that pay for government and commercial infrastructure, along with whatever services are provided to the people to manage resistance and resentment. Publicly borrowed money spent on privatized national priorities are capitalized as treasury bonds that affluent speculators purchase and profit from.

The formula Hamilton created is simple enough. The governing propertied class borrows in the name of the people to pay for everything from wars to subsidies for their corporations. They use the loans for their own ends, buy up interest-accumulating bonds created to capitalize the debt, then make the people pick up the tab and pay both the principal and interest on the loan through perpetual taxes that require indentured labor over lifetimes and generations.

Hamilton put his plan into action by first proposing that the Revolutionary War debt should be assumed by the federal government. He sent his *Report on Public Credit* to Congress, and his measures were approved in the summer of 1790. Against the protest of states that had paid off their debts, the central government took on the debt of the other states and blended it in with the debt owed under the Articles of Confederation. The new Federalist government then assumed all of it as debt owed by the whole of the American people. With that, Hamilton also created a need to raise new revenues to pay the debt.

The Revolution had been fought and financed by both foreign and domestic soldiers and financiers. Congress rejected proposals to default on paying foreign debt and adopted a policy of paying speculators in domestic war bonds in full, with interest, in hard currency. But when it came time to honor IOUs issued to retired soldiers for their military service, the federal government adopted a very different policy.

The men who fought the British Empire frequently sold their promissory notes to speculators to pay their own taxes and debts during and after the war. When Congress suggested paying the soldiers at full face value for their service and reimbursing the speculators only for the purchase cost of those securities, Hamilton objected, and he got his way. Only current holders of the soldier's promised pay would receive full payment, plus interest.

Hamilton called this "redemption." The wages of soldiers who fought for independence was personal property, not privileged property. In desperate need of some income while they marched off to battle, they sold their government-issued promissory notes, and, in the end, they got the speculators' pennies on the dollar for their military service. A contract under duress promises no justice.

The intent of Hamilton's plan was to make the public debt a reliable generator of capital by making government securities attractive to investors and speculators. Creating profit for some from the public debt demanded general austerity, poverty to ensure the need for borrowing, and the full taxation of labor but not dividends.

When Hamilton proposed levying a tax on domestically produced distilled spirits in 1791, the Federalists' government was faced with its first domestic insurrection. Revolutionary veterans in western Pennsylvania had no access to markets for their grain crops. They made whiskey as a portable, nonspoiling product that they used in place of hard currency, which was difficult to come by. The imposition of the first federal excise tax brought families on the frontier to the brink of bankruptcy. Farms and land were lost to the tax collectors.

In 1791, the year the whiskey tax was levied, the citizens banded together and formed a militia. They blocked tax auctions of property. They chased tax collectors out. And in 1792, Hamilton prevailed on President Washington to send troops into the frontier to crush the revolt. He wrote the executive order himself.

It was the first use of federal force against US citizens. The troops marched across Pennsylvania against the protests of the Anti-Federalist governor, Thomas Mifflin. They were on a mission to preserve Hamilton's creditor-debtor scheme for raising capital. They were sent to ensure that speculators in government war bonds would continue to profit from their investments, and that average Americans would pay them their speculative earnings from the sweat of their brows.

TODAY, THERE IS LITTLE motivation for a government built to incentivize exponential property accumulation to step in to secure human rights when debt slavery is the engine of commerce, trade, wealth generation, and "progress" under capitalism. Law is at the service of the creditor—so much so that courts can garnish wages of debtors without their consent and transfer payment for the work they've done to the creditor. The debtor is a slave not only to the creditor but to the law.

In addition to barring states from "impairing the obligation of contracts," Article I, Section 10, Clause 1 of the US Constitution, in which the contract clause is embedded, declares that "No State shall make any thing but gold and silver coin a tender in payment of debts."[2] It was a promise to speculators and investors in government securities that they would receive full payment in hard currency from the public treasury and that debt relief policies would not be erected by the states.

Thomas Jefferson commented on Hamilton's plan to use debt as the engine for empire building in a letter to John Taylor, US senator from Virginia, saying, "And I sincerely believe . . . that the principle of spending money to be paid by posterity, under the name of funding, is but swindling futurity on a large scale."[3]

Two years earlier, Taylor had written that "wealth, like suffrage, must be considerably distributed, to sustain a democratic republic; and hence, whatever draws a considerable proportion of either into a few hands, will destroy it. As power follows wealth, the majority must have wealth or lose power."[4]

Today, contrary to common sense, the economy is said to thrive when debtors suffer and especially when they fail to extricate themselves from poverty. David Korten writes that "phantom-wealth economics values money more than life and organizes around the logic of finance rather than the logic of living systems. Phantom wealth economists are easily identified. They focus on financial returns rather than returns to the health of people and the rest of nature."[5]

In an interview with *CounterPunch*, economist Michael Hudson commented, "We called up the Bureau of Economic Analysis that publishes the GDP statistics. I asked what happens when the credit card companies make more money on penalties than they make in interest . . . The answer they gave us was: 'That's not interest. We count that as a financial service, and financial services are an addition to GDP.' So all the added penalties that people pay for falling behind in their debts for arrears are counted as a growth in GDP—as economic growth."[6]

Mijin Cha at Demos offers this basic equation: "GDP is a measure of raw economic activity, not a complete picture of economic progress. The formula used to calculate GDP is: GDP = Consumption + Private Investment + Government spending + Exports − Imports. GDP cannot distinguish between a positive economic indicator, like increased spending due to more disposable income, and a negative economic indicator, like increased spending on credit cards due to loss of wages or declining real value of wages."[7]

Economic indicators *can* reflect the financial health of commoners, but indicators on which national economic and trade policies are based pointedly do not. Domestic economic policies justified by GDP figures benefit extractive exploitation of natural "resources" too. The formula helps mask the hidden costs to the global population and future generations by counting nature's bounty as a limitless source of profit. Cha explains that

> Preserving the country's natural resources—essential to our current and future wealth—is not counted but exploiting them in an unsustainable manner is. Only when natural resources are sold or somehow commoditized do they show up in GDP calculations. For example, if all of the fish in the sea were caught and sold in one year, global GDP would skyrocket, even though the fishing industry itself would collapse and the broader ecosystem would be damaged irrevocably. As shown, our economic growth is increasing at a rate that cannot be ecologically sustained.

It's the policies based on this formula that continue to benefit a tiny minority of wealthy people. But it's not just a benefit to them; it is a revocation of the equality of all people and a measure of just how firmly wealth controls the governance of the nation and the world.

Cha wraps up by saying, "If poverty rates, inequality levels, natural capital accounts, and other metrics were taken into account as heavily as GDP, then different policies and priorities would begin to emerge. Instead, we are now focused solely on increasing GDP, even though increasing poverty rates, inequality levels, and other societal indicators show that in many ways, we are experiencing growth without progress."[8]

The irony is that personal debt is counted as an indicator of economic growth. The GDP counts personal debt on the "profit" side of the equation. This demonstrates the point that debt is the engine of commerce and empire—it is counted in the column of future profits to be made by cashing in on the indentured value of labor, which has been posted in the statistics as collateral owed to creditors by debtors.

Although debtors' prisons were outlawed in the US in 1833, it has been reported that President Trump's son-in-law Jared Kushner uses the courts to jail underprivileged tenants in his housing complexes when they fall behind in their rent, while at the same time collecting millions in rent subsidies from the federal government, all paid for by the rest of us.[9]

In the confrontation between the legal privileges of wealth and the unalienable rights of people, the law sides with the accumulation of wealth through garnishment, incarceration, and indentureship—in fact, modern slavery. Always, the rights *of* property give the materially advantaged power over the unalienable right of those without it to own the fruit of their own labor.

Wetiko over Honor

Adam Smith's 1776 blockbuster *Wealth of Nations* is regularly used as an argument for the kind of capitalism given life by

Hamilton. But Smith made no excuses for the propertied class when he wrote that "civil government, so far as it is instituted for the security of property, is in reality instituted for the defense of the rich against the poor, or of those who have some property against those who have none at all."[10]

The human spirit is capable of generosity, honesty, even honor. But the materialistic imperative to acquire more wealth at all costs channels an undeserving propertied minority into brittle indifference to community and human values. It encourages sterile rationalizations wrapped up in an "it's the law" mentality that makes it possible for some entrepreneurs to use their wealth like bait. They attract the poor to borrow from them and then trap their prey into lengthy if not lifelong servitude. Depriving the poor of the only asset they have—their own labor—creates greater and greater concentrations of wealth and widespread misery.

When they borrow, average citizens assume responsibility to work off their debt. Their ethical grounding in how to treat fellow members of society is a known human trait. Taking advantage of that honorable sentiment toward social indebtedness has become an acceptable business practice. The business of profit-driven creditors is to create an economy that traps people in poverty. There, they are vulnerable to financial blackmail of a kind that is today treated as if it were a helping hand offered from above. But the real effect is to establish a class of low-paid workers who will perpetually struggle to hand over their earnings as compounding interest. The poor, for much of their working lives, will continue to borrow back a portion of their appropriated wages to make ends meet. Those in need who turn to means of subsistence other than debt slavery are frequently criminalized.

Taking advantage of people with few legal options for survival is a dishonorable enterprise with deep historic roots.

Materialism and empire continue to sever people from nature and the land while forcing them into conformity with a legal system engineered for human husbandry. The imagery of debtors "getting fleeced" is apt. But treating other people as prey is both figuratively and literally cannibalistic, whether it is their flesh, their labor, or their minds that are consumed.

Native American scholar Jack D. Forbes wrote about the

> disease of the consuming of other creatures' lives and possessions. I call it cannibalism. Whatever we call it, this disease, this wetiko (cannibal) psychosis, is the greatest epidemic sickness known to man. The rape of a woman, the rape of a land, and the rape of a people, they are all the same.[11]

> The nice people in the offices, the typists, the lab technicians, the clerks and, of course, the owners, directors, stockholders, senators, generals and presidents who use, profit from, and feed on human exploitation are also cannibals to one degree or another. The most guilty of the wetikos are, I would think, those who mastermind, justify and profit from such systems. Such persons are the "master predators."[12]

Treating the resources of the earth as inexhaustibly extractable property may not feel like cannibalism to people from Western cultures. They don't see themselves as part of nature or see nature as a living entity the way aboriginal people do.

Peeking into the capitalists' pantry, we glimpse the gluttonous behavior of a ravenous minority that treats other people and the whole world as separate, unequal, and exploitable. The premises used to justify economic predation deserve scrutiny. In America, the Federalists' legacy has been grafted onto our brains to justify the accumulation of privileged property while making whole societies and the natural world pay the price.

We've inherited a system of law that justifies, legalizes, and constitutionalizes the whole swindle. That it is wrapped in a near replica of the flag of the British East India Company against which American revolutionaries went to war is precious irony.

Indenturing the Future to the Past

In 1789, the year the Federalists' Constitution was ratified without a Bill of Rights, Thomas Jefferson wrote to James Madison that

> I set out on this ground which I suppose to be self evident, *"that the earth belongs in usufruct to the living."* . . . Then no man can, by natural right, oblige the lands he occupied, or the persons who succeed him in that occupation, to the paiment of debts contracted by him. For if he could, he might, during his own life, eat up the usufruct of the lands for several generations to come, and then the lands would belong to the dead, and not to the living, which would be the reverse of our principle.[13]

Privileged property cloaked in corporate attire and weaponized by law has no scruples. When our children borrow for college and take on huge amounts of debt, they are being fed to the aristocrats running these profit-extracting machines. Economic profit without personal labor is the appropriation of the labor of other human beings backed by the legally protected authority to collect it. This system of debt servitude drives "progress," as Hamilton envisioned it would.

Student debt in the US for 2018 amounted to $1.48 trillion, not counting interest. That's forty-four million young scholars in hock and owing a good portion of their productive years to owners of privileged property. Credit card debt in the US for the same year was $860 billion.[14] Predatory lenders, by definition, approve loans even when the borrower has poor prospects of repaying the debt and the interest charged on time. It's a policy that extends the loan payments indefinitely and guarantees exponential profit.

Financial predation by property's international empire follows the same pattern as domestic predation. It's the struggling countries that fall victim to international lenders. Closer to home, it's minorities, the poor, the less educated, the elderly, and people in need of emergency financial relief who are generally targeted. Have a health emergency and no means to pay for it? You qualify for a loan from what looks like a financial institution but is really the front office of a debt-slave plantation where your hard work is the crop.

Often, crushing debt leads to litigation between the lender and borrower—or, more frequently, between the new "owner of the debt" and the original borrower, because debt is a commodity that generates profit and can be bought and sold. Although labor has been declared in US law to be neither property nor a commodity,[14] clearly it is both when a human being's obligation to work off debt can be sold and bought between investors. When it comes to a contest between rights *of* property and rights of people, litigation outcomes are predictable. Given the original bias of law under the Federalists' Constitution in favor of property over people, debtors generally get the short end of the stick.

Ghosts in the Machine

When victims of credit's predation get to court, the words of dead Federalist counter-revolutionaries like Hamilton and Marshall can be heard passing the lips of judges in every courthouse throughout the land. Attorneys dig deep into the grimoire of the law. They repeat footnoted spells and intone unctuous prayers to the blindfolded idol of justice. But Justice is gagged as well as blindfolded. She has no voice. She has been checked and balanced with the priorities of wealth.

Commoners fall prey to the lure of loans fabricated with impervious mathematical formulae wrapped up in the form of a private contract. In immediate need of financial relief, the poor sign. But when the oppressive weight of indentureship emerges from the math into their every-day lives, they discover that public law binds them in servitude to honor the private law of the contract.

They hire a lawyer, if they can afford one. They gather solemnly in court and plead their case. The séance is over when the Federalists have had their say. The controversy is resolved in favor of the owner of their productive future labor because the object of the law is to preserve the rights *of* property, not the rights of people.

Courthouse façades are scattered across the continent like a necropolis erected for the veneration of dead Federalists. The nation they envisioned, governed by the opulent, is safeguarded within those temples to materialism day in and day out. The law, interpreted by its robed ministers, consecrates property and anoints it against all transgressions.

CHAPTER NINE

Property's International Empire

Under capitalism, man exploits man. Under communism, it's just the opposite.

—John Kenneth Galbraith

Old Habits Die Hard

European imperialism caused the dissolution and genocide of whole cultures throughout the world. The history of imperialism, colonialism, mercantilism, and empire suggests that superior technology was what allowed Europeans to conquer and expropriate whole continents from the rest of the original human diaspora. But not until the meme of "property" infected the canon of law were muskets, cannons, and seaworthy vessels turned against the rest of humanity and the whole planet.

Most successful of the European empires was one with a self-aggrandizing name: Great Britain. It was a matter of enduring pride for an Englishman to say that "the sun never sets on the British Empire." Today, nations that once were part of that world-spanning domain—Canada, Australia, India, and fifty others—form the Commonwealth of Nations. To varying degrees, their postcolonial administrations emulate the British parliamentary form.

The United States is a former colony of the empire, but not a member of the Commonwealth of Nations. It broke its colonial bonds and declared its aspirations for a new kind of government based on the popular will and the protection of unalienable rights. Revolutionaries questioned the use of law to perpetuate excessive privileges in governing for the hoarding class. But the Federalists who betrayed those revolutionary aspirations conspired to impose a Constitution that differs only superficially from Britain's class-based model of government. As a result, the "special relationship" established between England and America in later years is best understood as a shared commitment to perpetuating aristocratic privileges for the wealthiest of men. Nations that emulate the British and the Federalists' systems of government share in that commitment.

The US Constitution established a tax-free zone for trade and wealth creation in North America. It removed trade barriers between the thirteen sovereign states that for a generation after the Revolution were a confederacy of nations. It abolished their sovereignty for the sake of unfettered interstate and international "commerce." It became a model emulated by new nations coming out of mercantilist colonialism.

It isn't surprising that leaders of the Commonwealth of Nations and protégés of American constitutionalism have been busy creating global "free trade" agreements to amplify the power of a minority-controlled worldwide web of wealth. But it hasn't been only ex-colonies of Britain. In *The Patterning Instinct,* Jeremy Lent argues that "especially since the mid-twentieth century—what had once been the Western worldview has now become the dominant worldview of those in positions of wealth and power who drive our global civilization, from Bangkok to Beijing and from Mumbai to Mexico City."[1]

The secretly negotiated "trade" compacts that they devise, much as the American Constitution, constrain popular governance over the uses and abuses of wealth in its many forms. These multilateral accords are more akin to contracts than to constitutions. They turn international law into a type of private law that can be invoked by wealthy parties and enforced by unelected tribunals. They facilitate the privatization of member-states' domestic governments and resources. At the same time, they protect the propertied class from democratic meddling by the rest of humanity.

Who Profits?

Qui bono? The underlying premises of international trade have changed over the centuries. Emerging from the age of competition for colonies among European nations, the nations of the world entered into merchantilist and protectionist competition. Now we are engaged in the era of corporate globalization. The underlying premise of this new international arrangement is the integration of markets, borderless exchange of capital, and relocation of manufacturing and services in pursuit of cheap labor.

The World Trade Organization (WTO) was established in 1995 and signed by 159 nations, replacing the earlier General Agreement on Tariffs and Trade (GATT), which had operated since 1948. Although there is a bit of language in the preamble to the WTO agreement calling for "raising standards of living, ensuring full employment and a large and steadily growing volume of real income and effective demand, and expanding the production of and trade in goods and services," it all boils down to opening new markets for corporations that are capitalized enough to engage in foreign trade. Much of the agreement focuses on protecting the equality of member nations and constituent corporate bodies. For the benefit of the global investing class, its terms seek to equalize taxes and duties, restrict domestic subsidies, simplify import licensing, and protect property rights, including intellectual property.

The Agreement on Technical Barriers to Trade (TBT) is part of the WTO regime. It governs and "harmonizes" domestic regulations with international standards. Regulations set by member nations for domestic products and processes, including standards for manufacturing and quality control, environmental protection, and safety regulations, are nullified. Standards secured through citizens' demands for the protection of customers, communities, and nature are subordinated to the commercial dictates of the WTO agreement, which places them into the category of "unnecessary trade barriers." The TBT is the international version of ceiling preemption, applied domestically to every state and local government of the member nations.

According to Ronald D. Rotunda and John E. Nowak, even though "the US Supreme Court is 'the most powerful court the world has ever known,' the Investor State Dispute Settlement (ISDS) provisions of WTO, NAFTA, TPP and other international agreements can supersede decisions of the highest national courts, including the US Supreme Court, and there is no appeal."[2]

The implications for the rights of people are substantial: the rights vested in property by law and the interests of the propertied class are well represented in negotiations over international trade policies and free trade agreements, whereas the interests of communities and the freedoms characterized as unalienable rights of people are generally seen as irrelevant to trade or are made the subject of "side agreements" to trade pacts. They are akin to the Bill of Rights, which were amended to the US Constitution over the protests of the Federalists and applied to no American but propertied white men.

The Federalists' example of vesting the right to govern within privileged property, such as slaves and corporations and allowing that power to be transferred through the objects of wealth to the owners, has been emulated internationally. On a global scale, the WTO plays the role of the US Congress in its capacity as sole arbiter of what constitutes cross-border commerce. The Constitution's commerce clause has been cloned, and public governance of the so-called private sector neutralized. Corporations, investments, patents, and copyrights convey to their owners the privilege of representation by trade tribunals. The effect has been the privatization of decision-making regarding regulation of industrial activities, environmental impacts, and popular participation at all levels. Local and state laws that conflict with international trade treaties are subject to preemption by unelected and unknown people representing the interests of the propertied class.

It's the Same around the World

At the height of what was prematurely dubbed the Arab Spring, US Supreme Court justice Ruth Bader Ginsburg said, "I would not look to the US Constitution if I were drafting a constitution in the year 2012. I might look at the constitution of South Africa. That was a deliberate attempt to have a fundamental instrument of government that embraced basic human rights."[3]

Justice Ginsburg rightly noticed that, unlike the US Constitution, which tacked on the Bill of Rights as an afterthought, South Africa's constitution made human rights a more central element of its frame of government. But can those rights stand up to the rest of the document's reverence for rights wrapped up in wealth?

Ginsburg either missed or was not concerned by the 1993 South African constitution's enthronement of rights for corporations. In a letter to the people of South Africa, Ralph Nader wrote: "South Africa's new Constitution establishes that 'juristic persons are entitled to the rights in the Bill of Rights to the extent required by the nature of the rights and of the juristic persons.' The American experience of providing corporations with similar rights that people have should ring alarm bells for South Africans concerned about preserving their newly won freedoms. While the US constitution does not explicitly afford corporations the rights guaranteed in our Bill of Rights, court decisions have extended almost all those rights to corporate entities, with disturbing results."[4]

South Africa's constitution is exceptional in its unapologetic recognition of rights for property. Even the US Constitution did not recognize corporations as rights-bearing entities until judges without democratic responsibility to the people saw things differently. Around the globe, nations have created other devices to arrive at the same conclusion: those who own wealth should be given exponentially greater governing authority than those who do not.

Mila Versteeg is associate law professor at the University of Virginia. While she was at Oxford, she reportedly read all 186 national constitutions enacted since World War II. She and her colleague David Law, professor of law at Washington University, have since studied those constitutions; in 2012, they published a paper titled "The Declining Influence of the United States Constitution."

The *New York Times* reported on their work, recounting that "in 1987, on the Constitution's bicentennial, *Time* magazine calculated that 'of the 170 countries that exist today, more than 160 have written charters modeled directly or indirectly on the US version.' A quarter-century later, the picture looks very different. 'The US Constitution appears to be losing its appeal as a model for constitutional drafters elsewhere.'"[5]

The *Times* went on to notice that nations replace their constitutions on average every nineteen years, which is precisely what Thomas Jefferson advised in a 1789 letter to James Madison, because "the earth belongs always to the living generation."

Asked by interviewer Rob Kall whether the constitutions Versteeg and Law studied gave corporate property rights similar to those for people, Versteeg replied, "I'm pretty sure that none of them do."[6]

Their research predated South Africa's 1993 constitutional language about "juristic persons." Nader got that one right. And he was also right to say that corporate rights can't be found in the US Constitution. But around the world, and in the US, rights vested in privileged property and conveyed to the owners of that property are common. They're couched in case law, statutes, and treaties, if not constitutions.

A global campaign to remove the power of public governance to exert control over commerce (redistribution of assets from the unbanked and underbanked to the wealthy) and the economy has been raging for decades. Even though matters of extraction, production, labor, and trade have direct impacts on everyone, they are more and more being codified as private and not public concerns. International trade laws and treaties around the world do for the global aristocracy of wealth what the commerce clause does for the propertied class in the United States. They privatize matters of legitimate public concern and democratic governance.

International law enforces virtually no direct governance over the use of privileged property, but places nominal obligations on nations to regulate that behavior. In 2011, the UN published its *Guiding Principles on Business and Human*

Rights. These "principles" were not binding on corporations. As voluntary proposals, they alarmed the corporate class sufficiently for them to trot out their lawyers and lobbyists to mount staunch resistance to any binding international constraints on corporate behavior.

The global battle being waged for the rights vested in property against the unalienable rights of people mimics US tactics for protecting privileged property from responsibility to the larger community. In litigation brought within nation-states, the central government and the wealthy minority hiding behind corporate property (and asserting *its* rights) are increasingly allied against their middling peasant class and the poor.

Neither the US Supreme Court nor any international tribunal is being compelled to subject the privatized rights *of* property to public law. Meanwhile, in America and abroad, the private law of contracts and the establishment of corporate safe zones made up of international treaties and reciprocal judicial accommodations are enforced as public law without public recourse or input. Business instruments chartered by public governments are born onto the global stage immune from control by the people in whose name they were created or the foreigners whose lives they wound.

Free Trade Is About Free Labor

Alexander Hamilton's scheme for centralizing ownership of land and resources and building an empire on the backs of the poor has been internationalized. Debtors around the world wish they had the same social and political rights as the people from whom they borrow. They wonder why the people with enough to lend have the upper hand in governance over those without enough to get by. Their curiosity was anticipated over two millennia ago by Aristotle, who said "oligarchy is when men of property have the government in their hands; democracy, the opposite, when the indigent, and not the men of property, are the rulers." (*Politics* 3.8).

The rancor over austerity programs being imposed in a growing number of nations echoes the outrage that followed two years after ratification of the US Constitution. As discussed in chapter 8, quick on the heels of Hamilton's imposing his antidemocratic domestic excise taxes to pay speculators in nationalized war debt, settlers in western Pennsylvania revolted. Historians continue to condescendingly refer to the insurrection as the Whiskey Rebellion. Modern media tend to treat popular uprisings around the world with similar disrespect, acting its role as moderator of message and defender of the status quo.

The story told to consumers of corporatized media consistently avoids mentioning that debt, as a globalized form of privileged property, transfers ownership of human work, community services, natural resources, and self-governance to the wealthy owners of debt. According to a 2012 *Economic Times* report, defunding domestic programs and public services that benefit the majority to pay the interest on national debt to the investing class is a growing international trend.[7]

In Portugal, the IMF and other European countries agreed to a financial bailout of €78 billion on condition that Portugal cut the wages of workers in public services, raise income taxes, and cut the military budget.

In Italy, where in 2011 the public debt was around 120 percent of GDP and interest rates on the debt were escalating, public salaries were frozen and public jobs were drastically reduced, pensions were cut, and health care fees were raised, as were income taxes for top brackets.

In the Irish Republic, a bailout of €85 billion by the IMF and European countries required a minimum wage cut for workers, a 5 percent cut in wages for public sector workers, a 25 percent increase in capital gains taxes, severe cuts to welfare and child benefits, a cigarette tax, and a water tax.

In Greece, austerity measures that met with widespread protest included spending cuts, a public sector hiring freeze, and an increase in the retirement age. The story is similar in Spain, Germany, the UK, and other nations.

In the United States, according to the Department of the Treasury, as of October 2018, the national debt stood at over $21 trillion. Deep cuts in social services, public employment, and infrastructure maintenance, as well as attempts to privatize Social Security and Medicare, align with the worldwide austerity measures driven by public debt. Public policy is being driven by debt obligations.[8]

In the United States, rather than framing such measures as austerity policies, political opponents of public services characterize them as "creeping socialism" and propagandize for their elimination. It seems to be working. Millions of duped Americans demand that the programs they pay for and benefit from be cut. The irony is that when public funds are withdrawn from social programs that benefit the majority, the retrenchment is justified by villainizing those with the least as "takers," and praising the profiting wealth hoarders for their investments in the future. But the funds withheld from public services are redirected to pay interest on debt, to finance subsidies and tax cuts for corporate property, and to further enrich the wealthy minority who have never worked for any of it.

It's Our Responsibility to Act

Any honest exploration of the network of laws that sustains the dictatorship of property will reveal that it cannot be reformed. Adopting new regulations or electing new leaders can't bring about the systemic change that's vital to our viability as a society and a species. Laws that encourage privatization, acquisition, and exploitation are sociopathic and antidemocratic.

The community rights movement has begun to take up the necessary challenge. It's a young struggle still testing the rationalizations of avarice for weaknesses and chinks. We face a global crisis that is too big for any of us to confront on the planetary scale. That's why we need to adopt a rational strategy in which each of us strives, in the places where we live, to wrest control from the legal and cultural machinery of raw greed. We know that greed will not surrender without a colossal fight.

We have few options. Daunting as the task may appear, our lives must be devoted to this struggle, because so many lives depend on it. It's our challenge to establish an economy of life and justice, and an end to privilege and exceptionalism for the hoarding minority.

The place to begin is in our communities. Following the example of hundreds of others who have enacted local community bills of rights, you can assert your community's collective right of local self-government, recognizing that it is a right limited only by an absolute reverence for the rights of others.

For the community rights movement to triumph, one hometown after another must take a stand and secure social and environmental justice for the local human and natural community. To change the world for the better, let's acknowledge that these goals have greater value than financial profits, and that we already have the authority to secure them in enforceable law.

Despite preemption, despite bogus case law claiming that corporate property has rights, despite constitutions written with the protection of wealth against democracy in mind, we share a common humanity, and as the living generation we are entitled to an equal but not greater share in the life of the planet. We are also obligated to preserve and sustain the dignity and quality of life on this planet for future generations. Action is required.

Community Rights Challenge the Dictatorship of Property

It is hard to fight an enemy who has outposts in your head.
—Sally Kempton

To REVISE THE FUTURE, challenge the past. Let the American Revolution resume! We can end the dictatorship of wealth through legally privileged property when everyone has unencumbered and equal authority to participate in making decisions for the communities where they live. It's time to pick up where Thomas Paine left off. We can, as he urged his contemporaries, "begin the world over again."

Knowing how wealth rules the world is one thing; deciding what to do about it is another. The urgency to make that decision has never been greater. Humanity has separated itself psychologically, intellectually, and ethically from the natural world. The human population has reached a size that is crowding out habitats for most species on the planet. We are exploiting the forests, soil, waters, and air in a way that is propelling us inexorably toward a great die-off of life. There is a growing likelihood that our habits of consumption will culminate in our own extinction. Doing nothing cannot be the choice we make. It's time for us, the commoners, the regular folk directly affected by governing decisions, to start governing.

James Madison and his Federalist allies at the 1787 Philadelphia convention worried that the wealth of the "opulent minority" would be "insecure" if a constitution establishing
democracy were adopted. He should have worried that form-
ing a government that places riches above rights would perpetuate tyranny. It's unlikely he could have foreseen the other
dire consequences of protecting privileges for the wealthy few
above all other things.

Rights in property privatize the law, mock justice, and
make abuse of women, minorities, foreigners, the poor, and
the whole planet into collateral damage in the battle for absolute control by the smallest of minorities, the propertied over-
lords of America and the world.

What can *you* do to help legalize democracy, protect unalienable rights, legalize sustainable communities and sustainable and regenerative rights for ecosystems? What is already
being done? Fortunately, we have some answers to offer from
a growing popular movement that is challenging the oppressive status quo. And you can be a part of it.

Historically, to secure rights previously denied, America's
oppressed populations and their sympathizers formed people's
movements to challenge systemic injustice. From the abolitionists, suffragists, agrarian populists, antisegregationists, gay
rights activists, and others, we have learned many lessons. The
movement to elevate the rights of people, nature, and communities above the privileges conveyed by law to a wealthy minority is already under way.

In the earliest years of the twenty-first century, CELDF, co-
founded by Thomas Linzey and Stacey Schmader, set off on a
path leading away from progressive strategies modeled on the
efficiencies of corporate management. They abandoned the
comfort zone of activism that is devoid of confrontation with
long-standing property-based legal doctrines. They were

joined by the late Richard Grossman, scholar, historian, and cofounder of the Program on Corporations, Law and Democracy. Together they explored the frontiers of what Richard called the "hidden history" of our nation. I joined that journey in 2004.

There was a consensus among our small, intrepid staff that the standard strategy of reformers—regulating harms—didn't satisfy the need to protect basic rights. At best, the gauntlet of regulatory hearings and public comment periods preserved the appearance of a public process. But in the end, communities across the country were being shoved to the curb like road kill, hit-and-run victims of a corporate state.

It was clear to us that when reformers try to improve outcomes for people and nature by being "reasonable" and negotiating with well-heeled abusers, they fail. That's because their interests get caught in the cross fire between moneymaking and common sense. The sad fact is, too many activists whose hearts are in the right place have come to believe that common sense means not asking for more than you're likely to get without an unpleasant confrontation. It's been a senseless strategy, a common error, and, most of all, a loser.

We parted ways with progressives trying to regulate the amount of harm people would have to tolerate within the existing legal structure. To us, common sense said there had to be a better way and that we had to figure out what that was.

My colleagues and I at CELDF made a hard decision. No more begging for a little less violence to our rights, our communities, and the environment. No more settling for nominal concessions and pretending they were victories. We didn't start out knowing exactly what to do, but one thing was obvious. First, we had to decolonize our own minds and get rid of historically dishonest but deep-rooted assumptions about American law and government. Then we had to share what we learned with people who were ready for structural change but weren't clear about what stood between them and simple justice.

Richard and Thomas developed the first curriculum for what came to be called the Daniel Pennock Democracy School. The school was named in honor of a young man who died in 1995 within days of exposure to urban sewage sludge dumped as "fertilizer" on a field near his home. Danny's parents, Antoinette and Russel, worked with us to educate communities about the dangers of this "totally legal" and state-permitted practice.

The school was a Howard Zinn–style "people's history" exposé of what we knew about the origins of corporate power and the America that exists, rather than the one portrayed in lore and legend. The curriculum has gone through a few revisions since 2003, and as of this writing we're working on new educational tools for communities across the country.

Although the weekend Democracy Schools were engaging and always generated personal epiphanies for people in attendance, we knew that deconstructing what went wrong in America wasn't enough. If we were going to be a think tank untangling the mechanisms creating social and environmental injustice, we'd have to take what we learned into the communities in our home state of Pennsylvania, share it there, and help people challenge the rules that make democracy and local self-government for the protection of social and environmental rights illegal.

We met thousands of regular people who were sick of being pushed around and forced to live with decisions about their hometowns that they had no hand in making. They didn't understand what was wrong or why it seemed impossible to get the law to defend their rights. We had some suggestions for them, and they shared their wisdom with us.

We started in the rural center of the commonwealth and heard from lots of municipal leaders and community members. They wanted to know why they couldn't stop factory farms from decimating their local agricultural economies, and why the state was encouraging farmers to use urban sewage sludge as fertilizer, even after children had died from exposure to it. They couldn't understand how the state could continue issuing permits to waste haulers to legalize the spreading of poisons. They were sure the practice would stop once the state agencies heard their testimony and read the science. They learned that science and facts don't matter when they contradict the imperatives of whatever Congress calls "commerce."

Here was our point of entry—an opportunity to talk with folks who'd been through the administrative meat grinder and been told there was nothing they could do. We explained how the law works and whom it works for and why it doesn't generally work for them.

Putting together a strategy to advance community rights grew from our encounters with people in communities under assault. We asked what they needed and what was stopping them from getting it. They helped us figure out the choke points that held local democracy and community self-government at bay. The answers weren't immediately clear, but we began to recognize, one by one, where the camouflaged roadblocks had been thrown in the path of democracy. We didn't know what we didn't know, and we had to free our own minds first, to be able to see through the American jingoism to the stark truth of our predicament.

Unwelcome but Needed Epiphanies

In the United States, law is predictable. That's because the premises of the law are knowable. But even though they are knowable, many of the "givens" that shape the law's underlying logic have been ingeniously hidden from public awareness for a long time. This book has attempted to expose some of the obscure rules that turn participation in the "republic" by average Americans into empty rituals of democracy without the substance.

There is a sense of stunned betrayal that's known all too well by people who take on the legal system to protect their hometowns only to find out the deck is stacked against them. Until you join the ranks of activated and battle-tested citizens, it's easier to believe that however complicated the rules may be, they serve justice.

Even repeated abuse at the hands of the courts, as they ignore the interests and pleadings of alarmed citizens, often fails to shake people's faith in American justice. A kind of Stockholm syndrome takes hold. We've been taught to revere the men who wrote the US Constitution. Criticism of that sacred document takes most Americans out of their comfort zone. Nobody says, "I demand a blood test" when the wealthy men who wrote the Constitution are referred to as our founding fathers. However, a lot of discomfort is generated by exposing the Federalists as counterrevolutionaries who are responsible for the repeated abuse of our communities and freedoms.

At CELDF, we concluded that it was time to develop a strategy that addresses the reasons we are powerless. Instead of taking one more swing at the symptoms of our disempowerment, we knew we had to stop conflating the Federalists' scheme for governing with the aspirations of democracy-loving American revolutionaries. That meant challenging everything, from the borders and boundaries that created a wall separating privileged property from community accountability, on up to the laws that make rights in things a higher priority than rights in people.

We started about where the folk challenging the absurdity of "corporate personhood" have landed. That's why our first foray into confronting the system that favors privileges over rights was to draft a local law denying personhood for corporate property. But eventually we realized that although it makes sense to end that legal fable once and for all, corporations are not our main problem. They're just the most familiar type of privileged property. No, corporations aren't the problem; it's the people who hide behind that privileged property and reap all the benefits from the preposterous invention of rights for corporate property.

My colleagues and I have worked with communities across the United States to write and enact local Community Bill of Rights ordinances, amendments to existing home rule charters, and entire municipal charters. We've been met by furious opposition from attorneys representing moneyed corporations, "nonprofit" industry trade groups, chambers of commerce, and monopolistic media outlets. They've joined forces to sue citizens and municipalities to overturn or keep off the ballot local laws protecting community rights against their for-profit priorities.

This cohort of the wealthy has had loyal allies in the courts, on boards of elections, and among secretaries of state. Still, our communities don't give up. They won't take no to democracy as an answer. As of this writing, proponents of county home rule charters and local laws that have repeatedly been blocked from ballot access for shifting and inconsistent reasons are preparing to sue the state of Ohio for violations of First Amendment rights and state constitutional rights to the initiative process.

So, what's the point? If the courts and all the functionaries of government are going to block and overturn all our communities' attempts to overcome the hegemony and dictatorship of property, why bother drafting and enacting Community Bills of Rights?

The short answer is that the struggle for unalienable rights is no place for those demanding immediate gratification. No people's movement in American history won equal rights for all merely by appealing for justice from the courts. It's not to be found there, even though the judicial branch is sometimes called the "justice system."

A few rulings by lower courts overturning local laws that protect unalienable rights don't mean a thing. Magistrate judges scrapping local legislation and imposing punitive sanctions on the attorneys arguing the case for justice won't stop the people from demanding their rights. When boards of elections block petitioned initiatives from appearing on the ballot, as we're seeing happen more and more frequently across the country, the members of those boards have chosen the losing side of history. The community rights movement is young compared with the struggle for racial justice. But there are strategic parallels.

Being lectured by the court that we've paid insufficient deference to long-standing legal precedent will not dissuade the drive for justice. Unjust precedent is unjust. It perpetuates injustice. We the People won't be governed by dead Federalists. We will govern our communities and not be denied the right of local community self-government.

Like the civil rights movement, the community rights movement's first job is to win the minds and hearts of the people. It's our job to expose for all to see the naked facts of official oppression. Using tactics like the lunch-counter sit-ins, the bus boycotts, and the local organizing for local needs, we've got to open people's eyes to see that it's not "all for the best" that small towns trying to protect themselves are not just

NIMBY-minded bumpkins that need to be put in their place for getting in the way of "progress."

Civil rights workers were accused of rocking the boat, of being too impatient for justice, and of showing insufficient deference to "the rule of law." When the law protects some but not all, and when it deprives every one of us our right of self-determination, that species of enslavement to institutionalized oppression must be challenged and overcome.

Community rights workers are sometimes condescendingly criticized by people who are as wrongheaded as those who fought tooth and nail against immediate desegregation and equal rights. Desegregation gradualists and progressive reformers alike advise against asking for too much too soon. But "justice too long delayed is justice denied," as Martin Luther King Jr. wrote in "Letter from Birmingham Jail."

The persistence of injustice in America is nourished by the habit of trusting the legacy of the Federalist framers over the honest plea for justice of each living generation. Alexander Hamilton may have been right when he quipped that the voice of We the People is not the voice of God. But he had no qualms about replacing the voice of the people with the opinions of Federalists, now long dead, and conjured again and again by the rule of precedent.

The Federalists' Constitution made Africans property. It counted women as nothing. It sanctioned genocide for continental expansion. It made the whole of nature into property with no rights. It gave rights to privileged property and allowed whoever grabbed it, by whatever means, to enjoy those rights. It took from the people any practical means to "reform, alter or abolish" government when it fails to secure unalienable rights. It stole from all of us the sovereignty over our own lives and communities.

Our freedom was not theirs to take. But it is ours to re-claim. The Revolution is far from over. It was betrayed, and our natural rights as free people were never firmly secured. They remain to be won. Accomplishing that requires that we strip away the pretense of justice and bring the chains out into the open for all to see. That's been my purpose in these pages.

We have no better place to start than to disconnect our-selves from the matrix of illusions and reconnect with the real world.

Gathering the Community Rights Movement

Tip O'Neil, the long-serving Speaker of the House of Repre-sentatives, famously said that "all politics is local." The true eighteenth-century American revolutionaries believed this implicitly. Community is the foundation of society and all legitimate government. But community is the very thing the Federalists stripped from us, and what their ideological de-scendants continue to hold tauntingly beyond our reach. We have the trappings of a democratic process, but not the reality. Reclaiming community sovereignty over commercial agendas is imperative, and it will require us to reject the ideological borders erected by the corporate political parties that keep us from crossing the street to talk with neighbors who vote for the other party.

It should be obvious that trying to escape the quagmire of history forces us to begin where we live and make changes there first. Some say that we'll need to begin within ourselves. That's true, no doubt. Escaping our belief in falsehoods must surely be our starting point. Let's begin that journey by over-coming every shadow of doubt that we have the authority, the right, the competence, and the will to challenge and overcome every obstacle between us and justice.

Having worked diligently to understand the true nature of our plight, we can turn to the liberation of our hometowns. More than two hundred townships, counties, boroughs, and cities across the US have enacted Community Bills of Rights. Hundreds of others have tried and been blocked by the predictable reactionary pushback of entitled wealth.

Those who tried and were met with withering opposition have gone through a transformation from which there is no turning back. They've become part of the community rights movement and have begun the work necessary to resume and complete the sidelined American Revolution.

A new democratic spirit has flowered from those communities that have engaged in rights-based campaigns. In New Hampshire, Ohio, Pennsylvania, Colorado, and Oregon, they have formed the new state-level Community Rights Networks (CRNs) and have begun the work of amending state constitutions in ways that will empower the people, right where they live, to elevate unalienable rights for their communities and for nature above the privileges that law gives the wealthiest among us.

Changing constitutions has been made prohibitively difficult for mere citizens, but routine for concentrated wealth. Nonetheless, there is no more urgent cause than bringing our state constitutions into conformity with the aspirations and consent of the governed. This will require new democratic processes for proposing and adopting rights-asserting amendments. And it means enacting the constitutional guarantee in every state that a right of local community self-government is a right that will remain free from state preemption and private challenge.

CELDF developed amendment language that's already gaining support in New Hampshire, Ohio, Oregon, and Pennsylvania. Here's the text of the amendment being petitioned in Ohio:

Be it Enacted by the People of the State of Ohio

In the constitution of the state of Ohio, add section 22 to Article I as follows:

Section 22. Right of Local Community Self-Government

(1) All political power is inherent in the people, all government of right originates from the people, and the people have the right to alter, reform, or abolish their governmental system whenever they deem it necessary to protect their liberty and well-being; therefore, the people of Ohio possess an inherent and inalienable right of local community self-government in each county, city, township, and village.

(2) That right shall include the power of the people, and the power of their governments, to enact and enforce local laws that protect health, safety, and welfare by recognizing or establishing rights of natural persons, their local communities, and nature; and by securing those rights using prohibitions and other means deemed necessary by the community, including measures to establish, define, alter, or eliminate competing rights, powers, privileges, immunities, or duties of corporations and other business entities operating, or seeking to operate, in the community.

(3) Local laws adopted pursuant to subsection (2) of this article shall not be subject to preemption or nullification by international law, federal law, or state law, provided that:

(a) Such local laws do not restrict fundamental rights of natural persons, their local communities, or nature secured by local, state, or federal constitutions, or by international law; and

(b) Such local laws do not weaken protections for natural persons, their local communities, or nature provided by state, federal, or international law.

(4) All provisions of this section are self-executing and severable.

Communities freed from the dictatorship of property are not a pipe dream. The petitions are circulating to place this state constitutional amendment on the ballot. CELDF organizer Tish O'Dell is working with the Ohio CRN in that campaign.

In New Hampshire, where amending the constitution takes a three-fifths vote of approval from both houses of the legislature for it to be presented to the people for ratification, the amendment, backed by the New Hampshire CRN, got bipartisan sponsorship in 2018, thanks to the diligent efforts of CELDF organizer Michelle Sanborn. Although it did not garner the votes it needed to go forward, due mostly to political maneuvers by party bosses, the measure was taken seriously and racked up 112 votes for passage—about one-third of the House. Momentum is building.

In Colorado, an early attempt fell short of the signature numbers to qualify for the ballot, but it was a start. Our allies in the Colorado CRN and the East Boulder County United group have been at the center of that effort.

In Oregon, the state blocked ballot access. But, guided by CELDF Northwestern organizer Kai Huschke, the community pushed back, and the Oregon Supreme Court insisted that neither the executive nor the judicial branch of government had authority to block the people, in their lawmaking authority, from proposing law through the initiative process. But that wasn't the end of it. Due to delays in getting a ballot title (the language that appears on the ballot) from the Oregon secretary of state, the measure became ineligible for placement on the ballot until 2020 at the earliest. Not willing to wait, Oregon CRN representatives have been lobbying the legislature for sponsors and cosponsors to move it to the ballot more quickly. The cadre of allies for wealth's privileges won't surrender their dictatorial stance easily, but justice might prevail so long as we persist.

The effort in Pennsylvania has begun. Sponsors are being lined up. Community rights organizer Chad Nicholson is leading the campaign to educate legislators about the right of community self-government, but there's lots more to do.

We're at the beginning of the beginning, as Thomas Linzey likes to say, but we are moving forward. Exercising our right to amend and alter the government through citizen-driven constitutional change is the peaceful and preferred strategy for overcoming the dictatorship of property. Changing state constitutions to honor rights over privilege and self-government over authoritarian rule can free up communities to implement policies of justice.

Eventually, federal constitutional change must follow. The National CRN is charged with laying the groundwork—and not to merely repeal *Citizens United*, *Hobby Lobby*, or even *Santa Clara* and *Dartmouth*. Yes, constitutional rights stored in "private" corporations must be ended, but a change to the nation's constitution must do much more.

Realizing that such a momentous change is likely years away, National CRN is also facilitating communication among the state CRNs and spreading the word across the country about local successes and campaigns. There is understandable concern that an Article V constitutional convention might be an opportunity for plutocrats to make things worse than they are. That's why it's so important to understand how wealth governs with a free hand under current law.

What Will *You* Do?

Every step of the fledgling community rights movement has brought new insights and new tactics to the effort to align law with justice. From its modest beginnings to its David-and-Goliath struggles with multibillion-dollar corporations and their fawning courts of law, the movement has learned from experience and, most important, from the people who have joined us in this struggle.

We've been cautioned by well-meaning critics who point out that we can't win legal battles when we challenge corporate personhood, state preemption, and other "well-settled" points of law. Those comments generally evoke history's lessons from the abolitionists, the suffragists, and the civil rights movement. Yes, it was once constitutional to own human beings, to deny women the vote, and to segregate schools and public accommodations based on skin color. It was once illegal for people with different skin color or of the same gender to marry. And today, as it has been since 1789, it is considered constitutional to deny all people their unalienable right of self-government in the places where they live because protecting privileges vested in property was the priority of the framers of the Constitution.

We don't anticipate winning in the courthouses any time soon. That will happen eventually, but we'll have to change a few things first. Correcting our state constitutions will go a long way toward helping judges come out of the Federalists' shadow once and for all.

But first we need to liberate the colonized minds of human beings who are so alienated from the world, themselves, and their rights that they seldom believe they can make a change. Once they are convinced that equal and unalienable rights are our common birthright, then the government charged with protecting those rights will be exposed for its duplicity. We've been working on that part of the project for about a decade, and our work has begun to bear fruit. We need your participation to make real headway.

Without firsthand experience of official oppression, it's too easy for the average person to live in denial and maintain faith that there is justice to be had through official channels. That is why it matters so much what you do beginning today. To bring about the changes needed and to take up the cause of the American Revolution anew require widespread involvement of people and communities across the country. Hundreds, then thousands of communities must stand against the Federalists' curse, denounce the hegemony of rights in property, and claim their authority to govern in the name of the people for the causes of the living and yet to be born.

A lunch-counter sit-in, a bus boycott, an unpermitted march for justice—these tactics were technically illegal. Now these actions are celebrated on postage stamps and monuments, but their radical message of disobedience to oppression has been co-opted.

Today it's said to be illegal for a municipality to protect the rights of its residents if doing so would violate the privileges vested in property and conveyed to its owners. We aren't waiting for the postal service to honor our actions on Forever stamps, and neither will we shy away from challenging oppressive law.

We need you. Your participation in the twenty-first-century revival of the American Revolution is essential. Let them turn the lawsuits, SLAPP suits, and absurd damage awards against us as they once used fire hoses in the streets. Let the dogs of legal sanctions loose on us. Let the industries we face down write hit pieces calling us out individually, smearing us as radical and extreme and naive. Our call for justice is measured, reasonable, and unassailable.

As you think about whether you should join us, bring two or three neighbors together to talk about your community's aspirations and ask yourselves whether what's getting in the way of the realization of those dreams amounts to the rights associated with property abusing the rights inherent in people and nature. If you conclude that this is what's going on, I want to talk with you. It's time for us to get busy. It's time for you to join the growing community rights movement.

Look, I know there's a lot to unravel. This book is intended to shine some light in the dark. By itself, a book won't change the world. *You* can. But will you? If the answer is yes, then we want to help.

Drop us a line. Let us know what's happening in your community. And if you've got neighbors and allies who feel the way you do, you've got the beginnings of a campaign for justice and community rights.

We offer education and guidance, workshops, lectures, film screenings, public speaker trainings, local organizing, lawdrafting pointers, campaign tips, and, we hope, inspiration. Our partnership with the National Community Rights Network and its state affiliates holds the promise of configuring a national people's movement for community rights.

It's up to you whether you leave your mark on the times. We have a big job to do. When we reunite into communities and reestablish our connection to the living world that this culture abandoned, everything will change. But first we must change. We can't remain complicit in the privatization of the world. We must reject the unnatural role of consumers and be willing to decide what will be produced, and how, and for whose benefit. It's time to cast off leaders and bosses and governments that imprison our communities with unjust laws, drawing lines of ownership and exclusion around us.

A privileged few own huge swaths of land and deposits of ore and oil and gas and water, along with commoditized ideas and titled rights to every invention, cache of information, and creative work. They have no legitimate claim to hoard and monopolize and leverage for power what belongs to the whole world and to no one exclusively.

It's time to resume the Revolution once put on hold. We must stir from the nightmare that haunts each of our lives and terrorizes the living world. By renouncing the dominion of avarice, we can become what we were meant to be: unpossessed and no longer dispossessed. In community with each other and in harmony with nature, we can end the usurpation of our fundamental rights and govern responsibly, freed from prohibitions against democracy.

Let's unite in this quest to find our natural place in the world. Everything depends on it. There's no time to waste.

Ben G. Price

Contact Information
Direct to me:
BenPrice@celdf.org

For CELDF:
Community Environmental Legal Defense Fund
P.O. Box 360
Mercersburg, PA 17236
(717) 498-0054
info@celdf.org
https//celdf.org

Notes

Foreword

1. Chuck Collins and Josh Hoxie, *Billionaire Bonanza 2018: Inherited Wealth Dynasties of the United States* (Washington, DC: Institute for Policy Studies), 6, https://ips-dc.org/wp-content /uploads/2018/11/Billionaire-Bonanza-2018-Report-October -2018-1.pdf Page 6.

Introduction

1. Charles A. Beard, *An Economic Interpretation of the Constitution of the United States* (New York: Free Press, 1986).
2. James Madison, paraphrasing Alexander Hamilton, June 19, 1787, in *Notes of Debates in the Federal Convention of 1787* (New York: W. W. Norton and Company, 1987).

Chapter 1

1. Mike Argento, "Protesters Arrested Near Nuns' Chapel at Atlantic Sunrise Pipeline Site in Lancaster Co.," *York Daily Record,* October 16, 2017, www.ydr.com/story/news/2017/10/16 /nuns-vs-pipeline-arrests-made-after-atlantic-sunrise -pipeline-protest-lancaster-co/768487001/.
2. "Rent-seeking" is an individual's or entity's use of company, organizational or individual resources to obtain economic gain without reciprocating any benefits to society through wealth creation. An example of rent-seeking is when a company lobbies the government for loan subsidies, grants, or tariff protection.

These activities do not create any benefit for society but merely redistribute resources from the taxpayers to the company." Investopedia, "What Is Rent-Seeking?" www.investopedia .com/terms/r/rentseeking.asp.
3. Usury: excessive interest charged in payment of a debt.
4. Garnishment: the legal taking of property or wages from a debtor to settle debt.
5. See Peter L. Berger and Thomas Luckman, *The Social Construction of Reality* (New York: Anchor Books, 1966).
6. Wikiquote, Talk:Francis Bacon, https://en.wikiquote.org/wiki /Talk:Francis_Bacon.
7. Wikiquote, Talk:Francis Bacon.
8. Jean-Jacques Rousseau, *Discourse on the Origin and Basis of Inequality among Men*, quoted by Stuart Elden in *The Birth of Territory* (Chicago: The University of Chicago Press, 2013), 1.
9. John Locke, The Founders Constitution, http://press-pubs .uchicago.edu/founders/documents/v1ch17s5.html.
10. Benjamin Franklin to Robert Morris, December 25, 1783, National Archives: Founders Online, https://founders.archives.gov /documents/Franklin/01-41-02-0231.
11. Morris R. Cohen, *Property and Sovereignty*, 13 Cornell L. Rev. 8 (1927), https://scholarship.law.cornell.edu/clr/vol13/iss1/3.

Chapter 2

1. Benjamin Franklin, quoted by Alexander Keyssar in *The Right to Vote: The Contested History of Democracy in the United States* (New York: Basic Books, 2009), 3.
2. Arthur May Mowry, *The Dorr War: The Constitutional Struggle in Rhode Island*, (Providence, RI: Preston & Rounds Co, 1901), 129.
3. Peter Linebaugh and Marcus Rediker, *The Many-Headed Hydra: Sailors, Slaves, Commoners, and the Hidden History of the Revolutionary Atlantic* (Boston: Beacon Press, 2000), 48–49.
4. See, for example, Laris Karklis, Bonnie Berkowitz, and Tim Meko, "Areas Cut out of Utah Monuments Are Rich in Oil, Coal, Uranium," *Washington Post*, December 7, 2017, www.washing

tonpost.com/graphics/2017/national/utah-monuments/?utm
_term=.01324aabd0ff; Tracy Coppola, "Devastating Federal
Forest Bill Would Clear Cut National Forests and Silence Our
Dissent," *Earth Justice,* July 14, 2017, https://earthjustice.org
/blog/2017-july/devastating-federal-forest-bill-would-clear-cut
-national-forests-and-silence-our-dissent.

5. Ronald Segal, *The Black Diaspora: Five Centuries of the Black Experience outside Africa* (New York: The Noonday Press, 1995), 37.

6. Thomas Paine, "Agrarian Justice," in *The Complete Works of Thomas Paine,* Vol. 2 (New York: The Freethought Press, 1954), 498.

7. Paine, "Agrarian Justice," 482.

8. Paine, "Agrarian Justice," 484–485.

9. Peter Linebaugh, *Stop, Thief! The Commons, Enclosures, and Resistance* (Oakland, CA: PM Press, 2014), 194.

10. Thomas P. Slaughter, *The Whiskey Rebellion: Frontier Epilogue to the American Revolution* (New York: Oxford University Press, 1986), 79–86.

11. Robert L. Schuyler, "The Framing and Adoption of the Constitution," in *The Declaration of Independence and the Constitution,* 3rd ed., ed. Earl Latham (Lexington, MA: D. C. Heath and Company, 1964), 100.

12. Schuyler, "The Framing and Adoption of the Constitution," 100.

13. James Madison paraphrasing Alexander Hamilton, June 19, 1787, in *Notes of Debates in the Federal Convention of 1787, Notes of Debates in the Federal Convention of 1787* (New York: W. W. Norton and Company, 1987).

14. Madison, June 2, 1787, in *Notes of Debates.*

15. Robert Yates's notes quoted in *Secret Proceedings of the Federal Convention,* June 25, 1787, Senate Documents, 60th Congress, 2d Session, Congressional Edition, Vol. 5402, United States Congress, US Government Printing Office (1909).

16. Madison, May 31, 1787, in *Notes of Debates.*

Chapter 3

1. John Adams, quoted by Garrett Hardin in "The Tragedy of the Commons," in *Readings in the Philosophy of Law,* ed. Jules L. Coleman (New York: Routledge, 2013), 554.
2. John Adams to John Taylor, 15 April, 1814, National Archives: Founders Online, https://founders.archives.gov/documents /Adams/99-02-02-6278.
3. William Blackstone, *Commentaries on the Laws of England,* vol. 2, "The Rights of Things," The Founders Constitution: Chapter 16: Property, http://press-pubs.uchicago.edu/founders/documents /v1ch16s5.html.
4. James C. Cahill, *Cyclopedic Law Dictionary* (Chicago: Callaghan and Company, 1922).
5. Madison, June 19, 1787, in *Notes of Debates.*
6. J. Allen Smith, *Growth and Decadence of Constitutional Government* (New York: Henry Holt, 1930), 299.
7. Yates, June 26, 1787, *Secret Proceedings.*
8. Yates, June 19, 1787, *Secret Proceedings.*
9. Beard, *An Economic Interpretation,* 175.
10. Article IV, Section 3 of the US Constitution declares, "New States may be admitted by the Congress into this Union; but no new States shall be formed or erected within the Jurisdiction of any other State; nor any State be formed by the Junction of two or more States, or parts of States, without the Consent of the Legislatures of the States concerned as well as of the Congress."
11. Thomas Jefferson to William Branch Giles, December 26, 1825, *Founders Early Access,* Rotunda, University of Virginia Press, https://rotunda.upress.virginia.edu/founders/default.xqy?keys =FOEA-print-04-02-02-5771.
12. *Waste Management Holdings, Inc., et al. v. Gilmore,* 64 F. Supp. 2d 523 (E.D. Va. 1999).
13. Scott Harper, "Trash Imports into Virginia Increase, Report Says," *Virginia Pilot,* June 14, 2011, https://pilotonline.com/news/local /environment/article_bfe248a8-51c6-55b0-ae43-ed72586b1b8d .html.
14. Dennis A. Walter, *Virginia Legislative Issue Brief,* No. 24, July 2001, http://dls.virginia.gov/pubs/briefs/brief24.htm.

15. More on this in chapter 7. Also see CELDF's *"Model Brief for the Elimination of Corporate Rights,* https://celdf.org/wp-content /uploads/2015/08/Model-Brief.pdf.
16. John Dickinson, "Letters on the Tea Tax, Nov. 27, 1773," in *The Writings of John Dickinson* (Bedford, MA: Applewood Books, 2009).
17. Jane Anne Morris, "Sheep in Wolf's Clothing," *By What Authority* 1, no. 1 (Fall 1998), a publication of the Program on Corporations, Law and Democracy.
18. Richard Kazis and Richard Grossman, *Fear at Work: Job Blackmail, Labor and the Environment,* 2d ed. (Philadelphia: New Society Publishers, 1991), 76.
19. J. Allen Smith, "Centralization and Popular Control," in *Growth and Decadence,* 195–196.
20. "Statement from Minnesota Sands on Frack Sand Ban," WXOW .com (ABC News), La Crosse, MN, August 1, 2018.
21. Beard, *An Economic Interpretation,* 176.
22. Megan Quinn, "Oil and Gas Firm Sovereign to Sue Broomfield over Fracking Ban," *Daily Camera,* April 22, 2014, www .dailycamera.com/boulder-county-news/ci_25615501/oil-and -gas-firm-sovereign-sue-broomfield-over.

Chapter 4

1. David Brion Davis, *Antebellum American Culture* (Lexington, MA: D. C. Heath & Co,1979), 14–15.
2. R. Kent Newmyer, "Justice Joseph Story's 'Doctrine of Public and Private Corporations' and the Rise of the American Business Corporation," *DePaul Law Review* 25, no. 4 (1976), 826.
3. Newmyer, "Justice Joseph," 825, 826.
4. Newmyer, "Justice Joseph," 827.
5. Newmyer, "Justice Joseph," 828.
6. Newmyer, "Justice Joseph," 828.
7. An *ex parte* communication "occurs when a party to a case, or someone involved with a party, talks or writes to or otherwise communicates directly with the judge about the issues in the case without the other parties' knowledge." Hawai'i State

Judiciary (n.d.), http://www.courts.state.hi.us/self-help/exparte/ex_parte_contact.

8. Newmyer, "Justice Joseph," 826.
9. Newmyer, "Justice Joseph," 834.

Chapter 5

1. Albert J. Wolf, *A History of Municipal Government in New Jersey since 1798* (Trenton, NJ: New Jersey State League of Municipalities, 2004), 1–4.
2. Jon C. Teaford, *The Municipal Revolution in America: Origins of Modern Urban Government, 1650–1825* (Chicago: University of Chicago Press, 1975), 42.
3. Hendrik Hartog, *Public Property and Private Power: The Corporation of the City of New York in American Law, 1730–1870* (Ithaca, NY: Cornell University Press, 1983), 184.
4. Hartog, *Public Property*, 185.
5. John Forrest Dillon, *Commentaries on the Law of Municipal Corporations*, 5th ed. (Boston: Little, Brown, and Company, 1911), 154–156.
6. Nicholas Sakelaris, "Denton Frack Ban Spawns Another Bill That Limits City Petitions," *Dallas Business Journal*, May 11, 2015, http://www.bizjournals.com/dallas/news/2015/05/11/denton-frack-ban-spawns-another-bill-that-limits.html.
7. Nancy Burns, *The Formation of American Local Governments: Private Values in Public Institutions* (New York: Oxford University Press, 1994), 33.
8. Burns, *Formation*, 52.
9. Pauline Maier, *American Scripture: Making the Declaration of Independence*, (New York: Alfred A Knopf, 1997).
10. Simon Davis-Cohen, "Across the US, Courts Are Keeping Voter Initiatives off Local Ballots," *Progressive*, April 24, 2018, https://progressive.org/dispatches/across-u-s-courts-keeping-voter-initiatives-off-local-ballots-180424/.
11. Christiana McFarland, "Reclaiming Our Local Democracy," *CitiesSpeak*, April 5, 2018, National League of Cities, https://citiesspeak.org/2018/04/05/reclaiming-our-local-democracy/.

12. Robert L. Brunhouse, *The Counter Revolution in Pennsylvania 1776–1790* (Harrisburg, PA: Pennsylvania Historical and Museum Commission, 1971).

13. Sir Charles Fawcett, "The Striped Flag of the East India Company, and Its Connexion with the American 'Stars and Stripes,'" "Originally published in *Mariner's Mirror,* October 1937, "Flags of the World," https://fotw.info/flags/gb-eic2.html.

Chapter 6

1. *Burwell v. Hobby Lobby Stores, Inc.* 573 U.S. (2014) in which, by a 5–4 vote, the US Supreme Court decided that closely held "private" corporate property possesses the right to have religious beliefs and to be immune from regulation by public law when those beliefs were offended by the law.

2. James F. Epperson, "Selected Statistics on Slavery in the United States," Causes of the Civil War (2017), http://www.civilwarcauses .org/stat.htm.

3. Rob Wile, "The Richest 10% of Americans Now Own 84% of All Stocks," *Money,* December 19, 2017, http://time.com/money /5054009/stock-ownership-10-percent-richest/.

4. Thomas Paine, "The Rights of Man," in *Common Sense, Rights of Man, and Other Essential Writings of Thomas Paine* (New York: Signet, 2003)), 330–331.

5. Thomas Jefferson to George Logan, November 12, 1816, National Archives: Founders Online, https://founders.archives .gov/documents/Jefferson/03-10-02-0390.

6. James Madison, Detached Memorandum on the 1st Amendment, ca. 1817, The Founders' Constitution, http://press-pubs .uchicago.edu/founders/documents/amendI_religions64.html.

7. CELDF, Model Legal Brief for the Elimination of Corporate "Rights," https://celdf.org/wp-content/uploads/2015/08/Model -Brief.pdf.

8. For further reading on this subject, I suggest Howard Jay Graham's *Everyman's Constitution: Historical Essays on the Fourteenth Amendment, the "Conspiracy Theory," and American Constitutionalism* (Madison, WI: State Historical Society of Wisconsin, 1968).

9. Howard Jay Graham, *Everyman's Constitution*, 386.
10. James B. Weaver, *A Call to Action* (New York, Arno Press, 1974), 266.

Chapter 7

1. J. Allen Smith, *The Spirit of American Government: A Study of the Constitution: Its Origin, Influence and Relation to Democracy* (Chautauqua, NY: The Chautauqua Press, 1911), 286–287.
2. J. Allen Smith, *Growth and Decadence*, 190.
3. Alan Trachtenberg, *The Incorporation of America: Culture and Society in the Gilded Age* (New York: Hill & Wang, 1982).
4. Elbridge Gerry quoted by Alexander Keyssar, *The Right to Vote: The Contested History of Democracy in the United States* (New York: Basic Books, 2009), 23.
5. J. Bleecker Miller, *Trade Organizations in Politics or Federalism in the Cities* (New York: Baker & Taylor, 1887), 13–14, https://babel.hathitrust.org/cgi/pt?id=ucl.$b583552;view=1up;seq=1.
6. Samuel P. Hays, *The Response to Industrialism 1885–1914* (Chicago: University of Chicago Press, 1957), 95.
7. Martin J. Schiesl, *The Politics of Efficiency: Municipal Administration and Reform in America: 1880–1920* (Berkeley: University of California Press, 1977), 2.
8. Francis Parkman, "The Failure of Universal Suffrage," *North American Review* 127, no. 263 (July–August, 1878), 1–20.
9. Trachtenberg, *Incorporation of America*, 153.
10. Schiesl, *Politics of Efficiency*, 6.
11. See Adam Winkler, *We the Corporations: How American Businesses Won Their Civil Rights* (New York: Liveright, 2018).

Chapter 8

1. Peter Linebaugh and Marcus Rediker, *The Many-Headed Hydra: Sailors, Slaves, Commoners, and the Hidden History of the Revolutionary Atlantic* (Boston: Beacon Press, 2000), 49–60.
2. Article I, Section 10, Clause 1 of the US Constitution declares, "No State shall enter into any Treaty, Alliance, or Confedera-

tion; grant Letters of Marque and Reprisal; coin Money; emit Bills of Credit; make any Thing but gold and silver Coin a Tender in Payment of Debts; pass any Bill of Attainder, ex post facto Law, or Law impairing the Obligation of Contracts, or grant any Title of Nobility."

3. Thomas Jefferson to John Taylor, May 28, 1816, National Archives: Founders Online, https://founders.archives.gov/documents/Jefferson/03-10-02-0053.

4. John Taylor, *An Inquiry into the Principles and Policy of the Government of the United States* (Fredericksburg, VA.: Green and Cady, 1814), https://oll.libertyfund.org/titles/1308.

5. David C. Korten, *When Corporations Rule the World,* 20th anniversary ed. (Oakland, CA: Berrett-Koehler, 2015), 339.

6. Michael Hudson, "Modern-Day Debtors' Prisons and Debt in Antiquity," *CounterPunch,* March 22, 2018, www.counterpunch.org/2018/03/22/modern-day-debtors-prisons-and-debt-in-antiquity/.

7. Mijin Cha, "What's Missing from GDP?" Demos (January 29, 2013), www.demos.org/publication/whats-missing-gdp.

8. Mijin Cha, "What's Missing from GDP?"

9. Doug Donovan, "Jared Kushner's Firm Seeks Arrest of Maryland Tenants to Collect Debt," *Baltimore Sun,* August 16, 2017, www.baltimoresun.com/news/maryland/investigations/bs-md-kushner-arrests-20170812-story.html.

10. Adam Smith, *Wealth of Nations,* book 5, chap. 1, www.marxists.org/reference/archive/smith-adam/works/wealth-of-nations/book05/ch01b.htm, pt.

11. Jack D. Forbes, *Columbus and Other Cannibals* (New York: Seven Stories Press, 2008), xvi.

12. Jack D. Forbes, *Columbus,* 68.

13. Thomas Jefferson to James Madison, September 6, 1789, National Archives: Founders Online, https://founders.archives.gov/documents/Madison/01-12-02-0248.

14. "A Look at the Shocking Student Loan Debt Statistics for 2018," Student Loan Hero (May 1, 2018), https://studentloanhero.com/student-loan-debt-statistics/.

15. Edwin E. Witte, "The Doctrine That Labor Is a Commodity," *Annals of the American Academy of Political and Social Science,*

69, 133, https://journals.sagepub.com/doi/10.1177/0002716217
06900117.

Chapter 9

1. Jeremy Lent, *The Patterning Instinct: A Cultural History of Humanity's Search for Meaning* (Amherst, NY: Prometheus Books, 2017), 20.
2. John E. Nowak and Ronald D. Rotunda, *Treatise on Constitutional Law: Substance and Procedure,* 5th ed. (Toronto, Canada: Thomson-Reuters-West, 2012).
3. Interview on Egypt's Al-Hayat TV, January 30, 2012, www.memri.org/tv/us-supreme-court-justice-ruth-bader-ginsburg-egyptians-look-constitutions-south-africa-or-canada.
4. Ralph Nader to the People of South Africa, June 19, 1996, New Chautauqua Shakeout: Tools for the Countercoup, www.nancho.net/corperson/cpnadrsa.html.
5. Adam Liptak, " 'We the People' Loses Appeal with People around the World," *New York Times,* February 6, 2012, www.nytimes.com/2012/02/07/us/we-the-people-loses-appeal-with-people-around-the-world.html.
6. Rob Kall, "Is the USA the Only Nation in the World with Corporate Personhood?" *Huffington Post Blog,* February 8, 2012, www.huffingtonpost.com/rob-kall/is-the-usa-the-only-natio_b_1262525.html.
7. Mishita Mehra, "A Look at Countries with Most Severe Austerity Measures and Ramifications," *Economic Times,* June 5, 2012, https://economictimes.indiatimes.com/news/international/a-look-at-countries-with-most-severe-austerity-measures-and-ramifications/articleshow/13846767.cms.
8. US Department of the Treasury, "Monthly Statement of the Public Debt of the United States: Table I—Summary of Treasury Securities Outstanding, October 31, 2018, www.treasurydirect.gov/govt/reports/pd/mspd/2018/opds102018.pdf.

Acknowledgments

I am grateful for the inspiration and lessons learned from my friends and colleagues at the Community Environmental Legal Defense Fund (CELDF). If not for Stacey Schmader and Thomas Linzey, cofounders of CELDF, this book would not exist. To Thomas, our executive director, a big thank you for steering our adventure through the Scylla and Charybdis of a legal system as voracious and mindless as those mythic vortexes navigated by Odysseus.

I have fond memories and respect for our late friend and mentor, Richard Grossman, who dug deep into the mass grave where inconvenient historical truths are buried and came back with evidence of wrongdoing unimagined by the living. He told me that when he and Thomas invited me to join them, after my long years of corporate drudgery—and I accepted—I had undergone a mitzvah: in this case he meant a crucial life-changing event. Today I know what he meant.

Over the years our numbers grew, and our lonely quest became less forlorn. Gail Darrell joined us to begin community rights organizing in New Hampshire. Simple meals with her and her husband, Doug, in their Barnstead home, hearts speaking to inform our heads, gave new depth to our work. Gail was taken from us years too soon.

Mari Margil, our associate director, has become a global leader in the movement for the rights of nature. Mari has traveled the world to meet with advocates for nature's rights. Chad Nicholson, Tish O'Dell, Kai Huschke, and Michelle Sanborn are our Pennsylvania, Ohio, Northwestern, and New Hampshire community rights organizers respectively. They are the lifeblood of this work. Educators, inspirers, friends, and confidants to the intrepid communities that have become part of the community rights movement, they are beacons of integrity, empathy, and wisdom. I am very fortunate to have them at my back.

Thanks to Lindsey, Dan, Terry, Elizabeth, Karen, and many others from our legal team, and to Shannon Biggs, founder of Movement Rights in San Francisco. She's our California partner and longtime friend and ally.

I am grateful to Steve Piersanti at Berrett-Koehler Publishers for his encouragement and advice, and to everyone at BK for making this what I hope is a passable presentation of some far-ranging ideas. Special thanks to Shauna Shames for editorial and structural advice. Thanks particularly to David Korten for his helpful correspondences, suggestions, and generous foreword.

There are a few others who made this book possible through their patience, support, and encouragement. All my love and thanks to Kara Scott, my partner in everything. She is my confidante, advisor, friend, and ever true compass. My E.Q.

With love and appreciation, thanks to Andrew Price, my son. When I look to the future, I find inspiration in knowing there will be men like him with big hearts living in it. There are four others now part of my life who have contributed to this book with their patience and good humor: Garrett, Gabe, Gavin, and Grant. Thank you, guys!

I am also honored to thank my blood-brother Tom Mullian, a patient listener, always a cocreator and comrade in exploring ideas; without his lifelong influence I would not be who I am.

I am solely responsible for any errors or omissions. I connected the dots as certain social and historical patterns revealed themselves to me. My greatest hope is that this book will help us, even a little, to move into the future together and make it a place where we'd be proud to invite our children to live.

Index

A

Act 38 (ACRE initiative)
[Pennsylvania], 110
Adams, John, 47, 64–65, 90
Adams, Samuel, 47, 61, 80, 127
Adorers of the Blood of Christ
(Lancaster County,
Pennsylvania), 23–26
African Americans
Fifteenth Amendment
extending voting rights to
male, 140
labor of prisoners rented out
to corporations among,
151
segregation of, 124
See also Racial
discrimination; Slaves
Agrarian Justice (Paine),
55–56
Agreement on Technical
Barriers to Trade (TBT),
166
Alexander VI, Pope, 30–31, 32
American Civil War

Thirteenth Amendment
(1865) following the,
34–35, 75, 84–85, 125
as watershed moment in
ascending wealth and
power, 121–122
American flag, 120
American Legislative Exchange
Council, 116
American Revolution
Hamilton's plan to pay debt
of the, 152–153
how legal privilege has
hijacked the, 1–4, 16–18
justification premised on
values different than
Federalists, 148
Robert Morris's financial
support of the, 33
time to reclaim vision of the,
184
vision of local self-
government driving the,
114–118
See also United States

Anti-Federalists
    calling out those betraying
        the Revolution, 3
    opposing ratification of
        Philadelphia convention's
        recommendations, 61
    Thomas Jefferson's work as a,
        23, 61, 62–63, 66, 69–70,
        85, 90
Aristotle, 170–171
Articles of Confederation, 2,
    59, 60, 61, 69
Atlantic Sunrise pipeline
    dispute, 23–26

B
Bacon, Francis, 31, 32
Bastiat, Frederic, 1
Baxter, Judge, 100, 101, 102
Beard, Charles, 2, 68–69, 85
Bill of Rights
    corporations declared
        "persons" protected by
        the, 2, 18, 38, 75, 79–80,
        121–126
    Federalists' Constitution
        ratified without a, 160
    private contract law not
        bound by public,
        87–88
    the soul of the US
        Constitution, 4
    See also US Constitution
Black, Hugo, 131
Blackstone, Sir William, 65

British East India Company,
    59, 76, 120, 134, 135
British Empire
    American Revolution
        against the, 1–4, 16–18,
        33, 114–118
    continuing influence of
        postcolonial
        administrations of,
        163–164
    English common law of,
        51–55, 65, 66
    practice of promissory notes
        to pay war debt by, 153
    practice of using chartered
        corporations as
        "privateers," 134
Broomfield's anti-fracking
    ordinance (Colorado),
    86–87
Brown v. Board of Education of
    Topeka, 124
Brunhouse, Robert L.,
    118
Bureau of Economic Analysis,
    155
Burkhart, Ann M., 47
Burns, Nancy, 112

C
Capitalism
    cannibalistic treatment of
        other people as prey in,
        159–160
    Hamilton's notion of debt

fueling economic growth,
149–150, 151–154
Wealth of Nations used as
argument for Hamilton's,
157–158
Ceiling preemption
description and impact on
self-government by,
11–12, 14
Grant Township–PGE
dispute and issue of,
101–102
CELDF (Community
Environmental Legal
Defense Fund)
community rights
movement as central
strategy of, 109
contact information for,
192
Daniel Pennock Democracy
Schools developed by, 14,
178–179
developing a strategy to
challenge current system,
180–184
developing text of Ohio
amendment petition,
185–187
founding and earliest years
of, 176–177
Grant Township ordinance
against PGE's toxic waste
plan role of, 98–102
Lafayette, Colorado, Climate

bill of Rights and
Protections ordinance
(2017) work by, 147–148
Licking Township Ordinance
written by, 136–137
lobbying against
Pennsylvania's Act 38, 110
*Model Legal Brief for the
Elimination of Corporate
"Rights"* by, 129
Mora Community Water
Rights and Self-
Government Act (2013)
drafted by, 39–40
National Community Rights
Network partnership
with, 188, 191
Nottingham Water Rights
and Local Self-
Government Ordinance
role of the, 52–53
recruited to help guide
Ecuador's new national
constitution, 44
Tamaqua's ordinance
protecting ecosystems
drafted by, 42–43
Cha, Mijin, 155–157
Charles I (king of England), 115
Charters. *See* Corporate
charters
Citizen Tom Paine (Fast), 58
Citizens
corporations declared
"persons" with same

Citizens (*continued*)
   rights as, 2, 18, 38, 75, 79–80, 121–126
   current efforts to disenfranchise, 145–146
   Federalists opposition to direct legislation by, 105
   ideal of direct participation in local government by, 104
   need for community rights movement participation by, 189–192
· Whiskey Rebellion (1991) and first use of federal force against US, 153–154, 171
   See also Civil rights; Democratic rights; Unalienable rights
Citizens United v. Federal Elections Commission (2010), 17–18, 19, 122, 124, 188
City Council of Pittsburgh's fracking ban (2010), 14–15
City of Clinton v. Cedar Rapids and Missouri River Rail Road Company, 107
Civil rights
   contracts as commoditization of, 8
   corporations declared "persons" with, 2, 18, 38, 75, 79–80, 121–126
   floor preemption protection of, 11
   "Lancaster Against Pipelines" dispute and interacting, 26–30
   laws making property rights more important than, 82
   "right to survive" amendment ballot to secure, 8–9
   See also Citizens; Democratic rights; Unalienable rights
Civil Rights Act (1875), 73–74
Civil Rights Cases of 1883, 74, 95
Civil rights movement, 182–183
Cohen, Morris R., 36, 64
Colorado Community Rights Network (CRN), 187
Colquhoun, Patrick, 149
Columbus, Christopher, 30
Commerce
   Articles of Confederation on, 59, 60
   constitutional prohibition of popular governance of, 68–70
   global campaign over self-government and privileged property rights of, 169–170
   government regulations governing, 49, 72–76, 77–78

implications of engaging across state borders, 49

North American Free Trade Agreement (1789), 69

people at the mercy of corporate "commercial activities," 82

racial discrimination by businesses regulated through, 72–76

See also Contract law; International trade agreements

Commerce clause (US Constitution)

infringing on right of self-government, 49

invoked "for the general welfare," 73

Jefferson's letter warning about use of the, 69–70

proposed by Federalists to protect wealth, 68–70, 82–83

Waste Management Holdings, Inc. decision creating the dormant, 70–72

Common Sense (Paine), 33, 55, 57

Commonwealth of Nations, 20, 163–164

Communities

examples of recent state enactments subordinating, 110–111

how legal privilege blocks solutions to problems faced by, 5–6

an inclusive definition of, 40–41

international trade agreements preempting local legislation by, 118

left to enforce regulations with no power to make them, 80

New Jersey's Township Act of 1798 incorporating, 104

Plymouth, New Hampshire declaration (2018) for self-government of, 146–147

public opposition to establishing municipal corporations from towns and, 104–105

See also Local government; Municipal corporations

Community Bill of Rights ordinances, 181

Community rights movements

beginning with inclusive definition of community, 40–41

Broomfield's anti-fracking ordinance (Colorado), 86–87

CELDF's strategy centered
on, 109
Democracy School
curriculum developed to
aid in, 14, 178–179
first job to win the minds
and hearts of the people,
182–183
gathering together the,
184–188
by Grant Township over
PGE's toxic waste plan,
97–102
Lafayette, Colorado, Climate
bill of Rights and
Protections ordinance
(2017), 147–148
"Lancaster Against
Pipelines," 23–26
to liberate privileged
property, 40–46
Mora County's dispute over
fracking, 39–40
need for more citizen
participation in,
189–192
Ohio amendment petition,
185–187
our responsibility to
dismantle dictatorship of
property, 172–174
Plymouth, New Hampshire
declaration (2018),
146–147

Tamaqua government's
ordinance protecting
ecosystems, 41–44, 45
Community Rights Networks
(CRNs), 185, 187–188
Conkling, Roscoe, 131
Contract clause (US
Constitution)
Federalists' inclusion of the,
85–86
perpetuating debt slavery,
154–155
retooled by the Supreme
Court (1819), 88
as stated in the Constitution,
154–155
as tool for taking self-
government from
communities, 89–97
Contract law
allowing confiscation of
value from others, 36–37
City Council of Pittsburgh's
fracking ban (2010) taking
on, 14–15
as commoditization of
unalienable rights, 8
constitutional contract
clause on, 85–86, 88
Dartmouth case decision
making a corporation a
contract, 92–97
falling within realm of
private law, 9–10

as not bound by public Bill
of Rights, 87–88
See also Commerce
Cooley, Thomas, 113–114
Corporate charters
Dartmouth decision on,
95–96, 102, 105, 108, 110,
122–123, 138–139, 188
as "instruments of injustice,"
127
sovereignty of, 133–134
US Constitution seen as a,
128–129
Corporate personhood
Adam Winkler's
entertaining book on, 38
CELDF's strategy for
challenging concept of,
181
*Citizens United v. Federal
Elections Commission*
declaring, 12–24, 17–18,
19, 122, 124, 188
declared "persons" with
unalienable rights, 2, 75,
79–80
as a diversion from the real
problem, 124–129
Fourteenth Amendment
(1886) protection given to,
38, 74, 122, 123, 124, 126,
131
history of the evolution of,
121–126

Hobby Lobby decisions on,
122, 188
Licking Township
Ordinance (2010)
denying, 136–137
*Santa Clara County v.
Southern Pacific Railroad
Company* (1886)
declaring, 122–124,
131–132, 188
a timeline of legal decisions
leading to fictitious,
129–132
See also Unequal legal
protection
Corporations
British Empire's practice of
using "privateers," 134
ceiling preemptions
enforced through
litigation by, 12, 14
*Citizens United v. Federal
Elections Commission* on
campaign contributions
by, 17–18, 19, 122, 124, 188
Civil Rights Cases of 1883
review shielding
discrimination by, 74–75,
95
Dartmouth case decision's
making corporations a
contract, 92–97, 102, 105,
108, 111, 122–123, 138–
139, 188

Corporations (*continued*)
    Dartmouth College by the
        king as pre-Revolution,
        91–92
    influence on elections and
        legislation by, 83–84
    "Lancaster Against Pipelines"
        dispute over eminent
        domain by a, 23–26
    Lehigh Coal and Navigation
        Corporation's plan to
        dump toxic waste, 42–43
    Minnesota Sands' lawsuit
        against Winona County
        mining ban, 79–80
    Mora County's dispute over
        fracking with a, 39–40
    Nestlé Corporation, 52
    Pennsylvania General
        Energy (PGE) dispute
        with Grant Township,
        97–102
    people at the mercy of
        "commercial activities"
        of, 82
    privatization of contract
        laws applying to, 9–10
    regulatory agencies as
        barrier between the
        people and, 77–78
    sovereignty of a chartered,
        133–134
    Supreme Court's distinction
        between public and
        private, 90
    true American
        revolutionaries
        understood the oppression
        of, 127
    as the weapon of the
        privileged minority,
        134–136
    See also Municipal
        corporations; Privileged
        property
Corporatization of food
    production, 5
CounterPunch Michael Hudson
    interview, 155
Credit card debt, 161
Creditors
    claim to ownership of
        debtor's future labor, 85,
        151
    legal biases favoring
        property rights of, 8
    usury (high interest rates)
        creating wealth for the,
        151
"Creeping socialism"
    propaganda, 172
Criminalization of poverty,
    150–151
Cromwell, Oliver, 115

D
Daily Camera, 86
Daniel Pennock Democracy
    Schools, 14, 178–179
Darrell, Gail, 52

Dartmouth College, 91–92

Dartmouth v. Woodward case decision

  community rights efforts to repeal, 188

  Dillon's Rule doctrine made possible by the, 102, 108

  Judge Story's contributions to the, 90–91, 92, 93, 94, 99, 105, 111

  overview and significance of the, 92–97, 122–123, 138–139

  preemptions legacy of the, 111

  See also New Hampshire

Data mining/"private" surveillance, 6

Davis, David Brion, 90

"Death tax" (inheritance tax), 57

Debt

  Alexander Hamilton's notion of economic growth fueled by, 149–150, 151–154

  as claim of ownership of others' production, 149

  counted as GDP measure of economic growth, 155–157

  credit card, 161

  English "the terrors" laws criminalizing poverty and, 150–151

  student debt (2018), 160–161

  See also Public debt

Debt slavery

  Constitutional contract clause perpetuating, 154–155

  criminalization of debtors as modern face of enslavement, 150–151

  indenturing the future to the past, 160–161

  little motivation for a government to protect against, 154–157

  predatory lending that increases, 6, 161–162

  See also Slaves

Debtors

  creditors' claim to ownership of future labor of, 85, 151

  criminalization of, 150–151

  legal biases favoring property rights of creditors over, 8

Declaration of Independence

  Brunhouse's account on the adoption of the, 118

  challenging the existing law and restoring vision of, 137

  its message mimicked by the Federalists, 119–120

  "life, liberty and property" replaced by "pursuit of happiness" in, 63

Declaration (*continued*)
  reasons for colonists' revolt
    stated in the, 114
  "Spirit of '76" reflected in
    the, 3
  unalienable rights bestowed
    by the, 3, 21–22, 62–63
  vision of self-government in
    the, 114–118
"The Declining Influence of the
  United States
  Constitution" (Versteeg
  and Law), 168
Democracy
  Aristotle's description of the
    oligarchy vs., 170–171
  Federalist' efforts to subvert,
    1–4, 16–18, 19, 29–30,
    64–65, 66
  history of diminishing
    returns on, 142–145
  John Adams's lack of faith in,
    64–65
  See also Self-government
    right
Democracy Schools, 114,
  178–179
Democratic rights
  *Citizens United v. Federal
    Elections Commission*
    (2010) impact on, 17–18,
    19, 122, 124, 188
  current efforts to
    disenfranchise citizens
    threat to, 145–146

Dorr War (1841–1842)
  fought over property
    requirements for, 49–51
  extending voting rights to
    first male blacks and then
    all women, 140
  Franklin's jackass anecdote
    on property vs. men and
    the, 48, 50
  how ceiling preemption has
    reduced, 11–12, 14
  how legal privilege has
    hijacked, 1–4, 16–18
  "sacrifice zone" removal of,
    100
  three-fifths clause increasing
    the wealthy's, 16–17,
    82–83, 125, 126
  See also Citizens; Civil
    rights; Self-government
    right
Dhuaime's Law Dictionary, 107
Dickinson, John, 62, 76
Dictatorship of property
  description and why it is a
    problem, 4–10
  historic development by the
    Federalists of the, 1–4,
    16–18, 19, 29–30
  international consequences
    of the US, 19–20
  introduction to the, 1–2
  our responsibility to
    dismantle the, 172–174
  planetary emancipation

movement to free us
from, 20–22
protected by Supreme Court
interpretations, 4–10,
17–18
wealth accumulation
protected by the, 4–10
See also Privileged property;
Property
Diggers movement (England),
115
Dillon, John Forest, 107, 108,
109, 113
Dillon's Rule
the anti-Dillon argument
against, 113–114
boundless cynicism of
proponents of the, 111
as form of private law
enforced as public law,
108–109
Grant Township's
Community Bill of Rights
overturned due to, 102
historical evolution of,
103–108, 140
limiting authority of
municipal corporations,
107–109, 140
simple definition of, 107
on state subordination of
local government, 11
used by propertied minority
to upend self-government,
14

Doctrine of Discovery (Pope
Alexander VI), 31
Domhoff, William, G., 138
Dorr, Thomas, 49, 50, 142
Dorr War (1841–1842),
49–51

E
East Boulder County United,
187
East India Company (Great
Britain), 59, 76, 120, 134,
135
East Run Hellbenders Society
(Pennsylvania), 98, 100,
101
Economic growth
debts counted as GDP
measure of, 155–157
Hamilton's notion of debt
fueling, 149–150,
151–154
Hamilton's plan for public
debt to generate, 153
*An Economic Interpretation of
the Constitution of the
United States* (Beard), 2
Economic Times report (2012),
171
Ecosystems
Pittsburgh's "no fracking"
Community Bill of Rights
protecting, 44–45
property status under
Western law of, 42–43

Ecosystems (*continued*)
Tamaqua ordinance
protecting land and,
41–44
Ecuador's new national
constitution, 44
"Efficiencies of scale," 51
Elections
Citizens United (2010)
decision on campaign
contributions for, 17–18,
19, 122, 124, 188
Constitution's three-fifths
clause impact on early,
16–17, 82–83, 125, 126
corporate influence on
legislation and, 83–84
Electoral College, 83
Elite class. *See* Propertied class
Eminent domain
description of, 24
injustice of official misuse
of, 27–28
"Lancaster Against
Pipelines" dispute over,
23–26
Enclosures of public land
Agrarian Justice (Paine)
proposing reversal of,
55–57
British history of, 51–55, 150
Nottingham Water Rights
and Local Self-
Government Ordinance
to prevent, 52–53

English common law
history of confiscation of
human labor using, 53–55
history of enclosure of the
commons by, 51–55, 150
regard for private property
by, 65
Thomas Jefferson's argument
against importing, 66
See also The law
Environment
Lafayette, Colorado, Climate
bill of Rights and
Protections ordinance
(2017), 147–148
Pittsburgh's "no fracking"
Community Bill of Rights
protecting the, 44–45
Plymouth, New Hampshire
declaration (2018) on
protecting, 146–147
privatizing decision about
rate of destruction of, 76
Tamaqua ordinance
protecting land and the,
41–44
See also Fracking; Nature;
Toxic trespass (private
poisoning of the public);
Water resources
Epperson, James F., 126
Equal protection
Civil Rights Act (1875)
intended to provide,
73–74

Civil Rights Cases of 1883
    review failure of, 74–75, 95
myth of equality before the
    law, 37–40
European immigration,
    142–143

F
Factory farms, 6
"The Failure of Universal
    Suffrage" (Parkman),
    144
Fast, Howard, 58
Federal Energy Regulatory
    Commission (FERC), 24
Federal government
    ceiling preemption of
        lower-level government
        by, 11–12, 14
    making it serve the
        governed, 12–15
    rent subsidies from the, 157
    Whiskey Rebellion (1991)
        and first use of force
        against US citizens by,
        153–154, 171
    See also Government
Federal judiciary
    following the Federalists,
        148
    giving no relief to victims of
        predatory lending, 161–162
    post-Civil War political
        paybacks transforming,
        121

unwelcome but needed
    epiphanies about the law
    and, 179–184
    See also US Supreme Court
Federalist No. 53, 105
Federalists
    Articles of Confederation
        disposed of by the, 2, 59,
        60, 61
    commerce clause proposed
        by the, 49, 68–70, 82–83
    Dartmouth case decision
        victory by, 92–97, 102,
        105, 108, 111, 122–123,
        138–139, 188
    the Declaration of
        Independence message
        mimicked by the, 118–119
    falsely remembered as
        "founding fathers," 119
    the Hamilton musical giving
        misappropriated
        legitimacy to, 151
    House of Representatives
        and Electoral College
        established by, 83
    the legacy of injustice of the,
        183
    Madison's Virginia Plan
        accepted by, 62
    opposition to direct
        legislation by citizens, 105
    Philadelphia convention
        (1787) of the, 60–61, 65,
        67, 142, 176

Federalists (*continued*)
on possession of wealth
legitimizing aristocracy,
67
quasi-monarchical judiciary
established by, 3
Revolutionary values as very
different than those of,
148
subversion of democracy
and protection of wealth
accumulation by, 1–4,
16–18, 19, 29–30, 64–65,
66, 116
their counterrevolution
under Andrew Jackson's
presidency, 91
three-fifths clause pushed
through by the, 16–17,
82–83, 125, 126
Fellowship of the Brotherhood
of Saint Christopher of
the Waterbearers of
London, 51
Fifteenth Amendment (US
Constitution), 140
Fifth Amendment (US
Constitution), 87
First Amendment (US
Constitution), 87, 125,
133, 181
Floor preemption, 11
Food protection
corporatization, 5
Forbes, Jack D., 159

*Fort Gratiot Sanitary Landfill,
Inc. v. Michigan
Department of National
Resources,* 71
"Founding fathers"
collective false memory of
Federalists as, 119
hidden agenda on property
and land ownership,
58–61
popular history on the, 3
refusal to accept community
self-determination, 105
Thomas Paine not included
as one of the, 57
Fourteenth Amendment
(1886), 38, 74, 122, 123,
124, 126, 131
Fourth Amendment (US
Constitution), 132
Fracking
Broomfield's anti-fracking
ordinance (Colorado),
86–87
City Council of Pittsburgh
banning (2010), 14–15
Mora County's ordinance
prohibiting, 39–40
Pennsylvania drinking
resources polluted by, 98
Pittsburgh's "no fracking"
Community Bill of Rights
prohibiting, 44–45
privileged interests blocking
control of, 5

state of Texas ban on local bans against, 110

Texas House Bill 2595 prohibiting local restrictions on, 110–111

See also Environment

Franklin, Benjamin, 33–34, 47, 48, 50

Free speech right, 133

French and Indian War, 58

G

Galbraith, John Kenneth, 163

GDP statistics, 155–157

General Agreement on Tariffs and Trade (GATT), 165

Genetically modified plants and animals (GMOs), 5

George III (King of Great Britain), 58–59

Gerry, Elbridge, 142

Gerrymandering, 2, 142

Ginsburg, Ruth Bader, 167–168

Global world

community rights movement for liberating land of the, 40–46

how the Federalists' dictatorship of property system impacts, 19–20

internationalization of Alexander Hamilton's economic approach, 170–172

movement of planetary

emancipation to free the, 20–22

See also International trade agreements

Government

constitutional prohibition of popular governance of commerce by, 68–70

Dillon's Rule on local subordination by higher-level, 11

making it serve the governed, 12–15

preemption by different levels of, 11–12

understanding who it really serves, 10–12

See also Federal government; Local government; State government

Government regulations

administered by an unrepresentative bureaucracy, 2

of commerce, 49, 72–76, 77–78

"patchwork quilt of regulation" phrase on, 72

pollution, 76

used to deny right of self-government, 78

Government regulatory agencies

as barrier between

Government (*continued*)
corporations and the
people, 77–78
Declaration of Independence
on grievance against early
form of, 117–118
Interstate Commerce
Commission (ICC), 77
Grant Township
(Pennsylvania)
Community Bill of Rights
adopted by, 99
legal dispute between PGE
and, 97–102
as "sacrifice zone," 100
Great Britain
American Revolution fought
against the, 1–4, 16–18, 33
history of confiscation of
human labor in, 53–55
history of enclosure of the
commons in, 51–55,
150
Royal Proclamation of 1763
by, 58–59
"special relationship"
between US and, 164
"the terrors" laws
criminalizing poverty and
debt in, 150–151
Greek public debt, 172
Grossman, Richard, 42, 177
*Guiding Principles on Business
and Human Rights* (UN),
169–170

Gun regulation, 5

H
Hamilton, Alexander
debt plan to fuel economic
growth by, 149–150,
151–154
on "an excess of
democracy," 2
internationalization of his
economic approach,
170–172
John Marshall as protégé of,
90, 161
New York Plan of, 61, 66
predatory lending legacy of,
6, 161–162
role in crafting US
Constitution, 63
We the People is not voice of
God quip by, 183
Wealth of Nations used as
argument for capitalism
of, 157–158
Hamilton (Broadway musical),
151
Hancock, John, 61
Happersett, Virginia, 123–124
Hartmann, Thom, 129
Hartog, Hendrik, 105–106
Hays, Samuel P., 142
Henry, Patrick, 61
Hobby Lobby case decision,
122, 188
Homelessness

interests of the rich
conflicting with solving, 5
"right to survive"
amendment ballot to
secure rights of, 8–9
House of Representations, 83,
135
Hudson Bay Company, 134
Hudson, Michael, 155
Human rights
debt slavery lacking
protection of, 154–157
lacking in cannibalistic
treatment of other people
as prey, 159–160
UN *Guiding Principles on
Business and Human
Rights* (2011) on,
169–170
Huschke, Kai, 187

I
Immigrants' rights, sanctuary
cities, 5
Independent Petroleum
Institute of New Mexico,
39–40
Inheritance tax ("death tax"), 57
Injustice
charters as "instruments of,"
127
as legacy of the Federalists,
183
nine-tenths of the law
mathematics of, 82–84

of official misuse of eminent
domain, 27–28
See also Justice
Intellectual property rights, 87
"Inter Caetera" papal bull
(1493), 30–31, 32
International Monetary Fund
(IMF), 171
International trade agreements
Agreement on Technical
Barriers to Trade (TBT),
166
Constitutional tax-free
zones for wealth creation
and, 164–165
General Agreement on
Tariffs and Trade
(GATT), 165
Investor State Dispute
Settlement (ISDS)
provisions of, 166
local attempts at democratic
legislation preempted by,
118
negotiated by privileged
property owners, 20
system of law created by
Federalists including, 1
understanding who really
profits from, 165–167
World Trade Organization
(WTO) agreements, 68,
165–166
See also Commerce; Global
world

Investor State Dispute
Settlement (ISDS)
provisions, 166
Involuntary servitude
history of British
confiscation of labor
using, 53–55
Thirteenth Amendment
prohibition of, 34–36, 75,
84–85, 125
Irish Republic bailout,
171–172
Italian public debt, 171

J
Jackass anecdote (Benjamin
Franklin), 48, 50
Jackson, Andrew, 91
Jackson, Kenneth T., 112
Jefferson, Thomas
commenting on Hamilton's
debt plan, 155
Declaration of Independence
written by, 62–63, 115
declining to attend
Philadelphia convention
(1787), 61
on "the earth belongs always
to the living generation,"
169
on Federalists' Constitution
ratified without Bill of
Rights, 160
on his feelings toward the
federal party, 23

Midnight Judges Act to
prevent a Supreme Court
appointment by, 90
on value of self-government,
103
warning against importing
English common law, 66
warning against use of the
commerce clause, 69–70
Jefferson's Tidal Basin
memorial, 58
Jennings, Edmund, 65
Judiciary. *See* Federal judiciary;
US Supreme Court
Justice
dictatorship of precedent
over, 8
"Lancaster Against Pipelines"
dispute over interacting
rights and, 26–30
See also Injustice

K
Kall, Rob, 169
Katzenbach v. McClung (1964), 73
Kempton, Sally, 175
King, Martin Luther, Jr., 183
Korten, David, 155
Kushner, Jared, 157
Kyd, Stewart, 106

L
Labor
British history of
confiscation of, 53–55

creditors' claim to ownership of debtor's future, 85, 151
of prisoners rented to out corporations, 151
Thirteenth Amendment prohibition of involuntary servitude, 34–36, 75, 84–85, 125
"voluntarily" waiving rights to fair compensation for, 35–37
wealth accumulation through other people's, 84–85
Lafayette, Colorado, Climate bill of Rights and Protections ordinance (2017), 147–148
Lakota nation (Pine Ridge Reservation), 114
"Lancaster Against Pipelines" dispute, 23–30
Land
Agrarian Justice (Paine) proposing reversal of enclosures of, 55–57
British history of enclosure of the commons, 51–55, 150
community rights movement for liberating, 40–46
property status under Western law of nature,

ecosystems, and, 42–43
Tamaqua ordinance protecting ecosystems and, 41–44
Washington and "founding fathers'" hidden agenda on property and, 58–61
See also Property
The law
British history of enclosure of the commons using, 51–55, 150
comparing public and private, 10
the Constitution making public law private property, 61–63
contracts falling within realm of private law, 8–10, 14–15
created by the Federalists to protect wealth accumulation, 1–4, 16–18, 19, 29–30
endowing property with ability to convey rights, 66–67
how property is created through, 33–37
Jefferson's argument against importing common law into, 66
myth of equality before, 37–40

The law (*continued*)
nine-tenths mathematics of injustice under, 82–84
precedent used as weaponized rule of property, 65
unwelcome but needed epiphanies about, 179–184
See also English common law
Law, David, 168, 169
Lee, Richard Henry, 61
Legal privilege
for corporate property as "persons" with rights, 2
how democratic rights have been hijacked by, 1–4, 16–18
legal doctrines institutionalizing, 7–8
solutions to community issues blocked by, 5–6
Supreme Court interpretation sustaining, 4–10
Legislation
Broomfield's anti-fracking ordinance (Colorado), 86–87
CELDF's work on Community Bill of Rights ordinances, 181
corporate influence on elections and, 83–84
Lafayette, Colorado, Climate bill of Rights and

Protections ordinance (2017), 147–148
Licking Township Ordinance, 136–137
Midnight Judges Act, 90
Mora County's anti-fracking ordinance, 39–40
Nottingham Water Rights and Local Self-Government Ordinance, 52–53
Tamaqua government's ordinance protecting ecosystem, 41–44, 45
Voting Rights Act (1965), 75
Lehigh Coal and Navigation Corporation, 42–43
Lent, Jeremy, 164
"Letter from Birmingham Jail" (King), 183
Letters of marque, 134
Levellers movement (England), 115
Liberating the planet, 40–46
Licking Township Ordinance (2010), 136–137
Linebaugh, Peter, 51, 58, 150
Linzey, Thomas, 42, 136, 176, 188
Local government
constitutional limitation of commerce governance by, 68–70
Dartmouth private charter decision impact on,

95–96, 102, 105, 108, 110, 122–123, 138–139, 188

Dillon's Rule on state subordination of, 11

federal preemption of, 8

ideal of direct citizen participation in, 104

international trade agreements preempting legislation by, 118

making it serve the governed, 12–15

state preemption prohibiting law-making by, 8

Supreme Court's groundwork for privatizing, 90–94

"We wish we could help, but our hands are tied" lament of, 15–16

See also Communities; Government; Municipal corporations

Local regulations

commerce across state borders free of, 49

as substitute for local self-governance, 78–79

Locke, John, 33

M

Madison, James, 3, 59, 61–62, 63, 65, 66, 67, 90, 105, 142, 160, 169, 176

Margil, Mari, 45

Marshall, John, 85, 90, 92, 93, 96, 99, 105, 109, 161

Medicare privatization proposal, 172

Midnight Judges Act, 90

Mifflin, Thomas, 154

Minimum/living wage, 5

Minnesota Sands, 78

Miorelli, Cathy, 42, 43

Missouri River Rail Road Company, 107

Model Legal Brief for the Elimination of Corporate "Rights" (CELDF), 129

Mora Community Water Rights and Self-Government Act (2913), 39–40

Morris, Robert, 33, 63

Municipal corporations

Dillon's Rule limiting authority of, 107–109, 140

examples of recent state enactments subordinating, 110–111

founding of Grand Junction, Colorado as a, 112

Hendrik Hartog on early status and perception of, 106

historic decline of self-government by, 106–109

legal status of, 109–111

Municipal (*continued*)
opposition to, 104–105
proponents of Dillon's Rule
arguing state authority
over, 111
understanding that they are
for profit, 111–113
See also Communities;
Corporations; Local
government

N
Nader, Ralph, 168, 169
National Community Rights
Network (CRN), 188,
191
National debt. *See* Public
debt
National Labor Relations
Board, 133
Native Americans
burial grounds in Lancaster
County, 25
Dartmouth College
established in 1769 to help
train, 91, 102
Royal Proclamation of 1763
revoking land grants to
make peace with, 58–59
Natural Gas Act, 24
Nature
Pittsburgh's "no fracking"
Community Bill of Rights
protecting, 44–45
property status under

Western law of land,
ecosystems, and, 42–43
Tamaqua ordinance
protecting land and
ecosystems of, 41–44
See also Environment; Water
resources
Nestlé Corporation, 52
New Hampshire
efforts to amend the
constitution in, 187
New Hampshire Supreme
Court's *Dartmouth* case
decision in, 92, 94
*See also Dartmouth v.
Woodward* case decision
New Jersey Township Act
(1798), 104
New Model Army (Cromwell's
army) [England], 115
New World property lines
(1493), 30–31, 32
New York Plan (Alexander
Hamilton), 61, 66
New York Times, 168–169
New Zealand's Wanganui
River, 45
Newmyer, R. Kent, 91, 92–93,
94–95
Nicholson, Chad, 98, 147, 188
NIMBYs (Not in My Back
Yarders), 73, 183
Nin-tenths of the law, 82–84
Nineteenth Amendment (US
Constitution), 140, 145

Nondisclosure agreements, 87

North American Free Trade Agreement (1789), 69

Nottingham Water Rights and Local Self-Government Ordinance (New Hampshire), 52–53

Novum Organum (Bacon), 31

Nowak, John E., 166

O

O'Dell, Tish, 13, 187

Ohio amendment petition, 185–187

Ohio Community Rights Network (CRN), 187

Oligarchy, 170–171

Olivas, John, 39

O'Neil, Tim, 184

Oregon Community Rights Network (CRN), 187–188

P

PA Farm Bureau, 110

Paine, Thomas, 3, 33, 55–58, 62, 85, 109, 127, 151, 175

Paine'sWorks (Fast), 58

Parkman, Francis, 144, 145

The Patterning Instinct (Lent), 164

PennAg, 110

Pennock, Antoinette, 178

Pennock, Daniel, 178

Pennock, Russel, 178

Pennsylvania
ACRE initiative (Act 38), 110

Adorers of the Blood of Christ (Lancaster County) of, 23–26

community rights activities in, 188

Government Study Commission in, 100–101

Grant Township–PGE dispute in, 97–102

Pennsylvania Department of Environmental Protection (DEP) of, 101

Tamaqua ordinance protecting ecosystems in, 41–44, 45

"township of the second class" status in, 97

Pennsylvania Bar Association, 102

Pennsylvania General assembly
colony of Pennsylvania run by the, 47

drafting their 1776 state constitution, 40

Pennsylvania General Energy (PGE), 97–102

Pennsylvania State Association of Township Supervisors (PSATS), 97

Person status of corporations. *See* Corporate personhood

Personal property
description of, 6
distinction between
privileged and, 6–7, 33–34
unequal legal protection of
privileged vs., 37–39
Philadelphia convention (1787),
60–61, 65, 67, 142, 176
Pinckney, Charles Cotesworth,
62
Pine Ridge Reservation (South
Dakota), 114
Pipelines, 6
Pittsburgh's "no fracking"
Community Bill of
Rights, 44–45
Planetary emancipation
movement, 20–22
Plessy v. Ferguson decision,
124
Plumer, William, 91
Plymouth, New Hampshire
declaration (2018),
146–147
Police accountability, 5
Political parities
gerrymandering by the, 2,
142
pandering to ethnic interests
and machine politics,
141–142
Political power
American Civil War as
watershed moment in
ascending, 121–122

Aristotle's description of the
oligarchy vs. democracy,
170–171
Citizens United (2010)
decision implications for,
17–18, 19, 122, 124, 188
Pollution
government regulations on,
76
of Pennsylvania drinking
resources by fracking, 98
See also Toxic trespass (private
poisoning of the public)
Portugal financial bailout, 171
Potomac Company, 59–60
Poverty
English "the terrors" laws
criminalizing debt and,
150–151
homelessness and, 5, 8–9
Precedent
Fort Gratiot Sanitary
Landfill decision as, 71
as rule of property, 65
Predatory lending, 6, 161–162
Preemptions
ceiling, 11–12, 14, 101–102
Dartmouth ruling legacy of,
111
floor, 11
law-making, 11
Price, Ben G., 192
Princeton's History of
American Law and
Liberty Program, 105

Prison privatization, 6

Prisoner's rights, 5

Privacy right, 132

"Private actors" status, 76, 82

Private law
  comparing public and, 10
  contracts falling within
    realm of, 8–10, 14–15
  Dartmouth case decision's
    significance for public
    and, 92–97, 102, 105, 108,
    111, 122–123, 138–139,
    188
  Dillon's Rule enforced as
    public law even though,
    108–109
  how property is created
    through, 33–37
"Private" surveillance/data
  mining, 6

Private vote rallying, 5

Privatization
  British history of enclosures
    of the commons or, 51–55,
    150
  of contract and corporation
    laws, 9–10
  of decisions on rate of
    environmental
    destruction, 76
  of nature and ecosystems,
    42–43
  prison, 6
  proposed Social Security
    and Medicare, 172
  of public law, 8
  school, 5
  Thomas Paines's proposal
    for remedying enclosures
    and, 55–58
  water, 5

Privileged property
  British history of enclosures
    or privatization creating,
    51–55, 150
  collecting millions in rent
    subsidies, 157
  community rights
    movement to liberate,
    40–46
  distinction between
    personal and, 6–7, 33–34
  global campaign over
    self-government and
    power of, 169–170
  indenturing the future to the
    past, 160–161
  international consequences
    of the US, 19–20
  "Lancaster Against
    Pipelines" eminent
    domain dispute, 23–26
  legal doctrines
    institutionalizing, 7–8
  planetary emancipation
    movement to free us
    from, 20–22
  protected by Supreme Court
    interpretations, 4–10,
    17–18

Privileged property (*continued*)
  requires confiscation of
    value from others, 36–37
  slaves as example of, 16–17,
    82–83
  unequal legal protection of
    personal vs., 37–39
  See also Corporations;
    Dictatorship of property;
    Property
Program on Corporations, Law
  and Democracy,
  177
Progressive Era, 78–79
Progressive reform movements
  (early 1990s), 143–144
Promissory notes for war debt,
  153
Propertied class
  Aristotle's description of
    democracy vs. oligarchy
    of the, 170–171
  ceiling preemption
    protecting the, 11–12, 14
  Constitutional
    interpretations and legal
    doctrines protecting,
    4–5
  corporations as the weapon
    of the, 134–136
  the Federalists as privileged
    and, 1–4, 16–18
  other people's labor turned
    into property of the,
    84–85

slaves counted as three-fifths
  of person to protect,
  16–17, 82–83, 125, 126
solutions to community
  issues blocked by legal
  privilege of, 5–6
three-fifths clause increasing
  the power of the, 16–17,
  82–83, 125, 126
Property
  accumulation as not being
    an unalienable right, 29,
    33–34
  British history of enclosures
    or privatization of public,
    51–55, 150
  the Constitution making
    public law private, 61–63
  creating through the, 33–37
  Dorr War (1841–1842)
    fought over civil rights of
    men without, 49–51
  "Lancaster Against Pipelines"
    dispute over eminent
    domain seizure of, 23–26
  "legal fiction" of, 6
  opposition to "death tax"
    (inheritance tax) on, 57
  personal, 6–7, 33–34, 37–39
  Pope Alexander VI's historic
    division of global, 30–31
  precedent as weaponized
    rule of, 65
  Texas House Bill 2595
    prohibiting local

restrictions on economic
development of, 110–111
understanding the origin
and nature of, 30
See also Dictatorship of
property; Land; Privileged
property; Slaves
Property lines
"Inter Caetera" papal bull
(1493) creating New
World, 30–31, 32
understanding the nature of,
30
Property rights
"Lancaster Against
Pipelines" dispute over
privileged and
nonprivileged, 23–26
laws making them more
important than civil
rights, 82
legal biases against rights of
debtors, 8
shorthanded under the color
of law, 29–30
US law endowing property
with, 66–67
Protect Youngstown community
group (Ohio), 13–14
Proudhon, Pierre-Joseph, 7
Public debt
Economic Times report
(2012) on defunding
domestic programs and
services to pay, 171

Hamilton's plan to generate
capital through, 153
Hamilton's plan to pay
Revolutionary War debt
through, 152–153
indenturing the future to the
past, 160–161
of Portugal, Italy, Irish
Republic, and Greece,
171–172
US national debt (2018), 172
See also Debt
Public law
ceiling preemption as
privatization of public
authority and, 11–12, 14
comparing private and, 10
the Constitution making
public law private
property, 61–63
contract law as not bound
by, 87–88
Dartmouth case decision's
significance for private
and, 92–97, 102, 105, 108,
111, 122–123, 138–139, 188
Dillon's Rule as form of
private law enforced as,
108–109
how property is created
through, 33–37
Lancaster County's dispute
over eminent domain,
23–26
privatization of, 8

Public law (*continued*)
  timeline of corporate
    enhanced Bill of Rights
    immunities from, 129–132

R
Racial discrimination
  *Brown v. Board of Education
    of Topeka* prohibition of
    segregation, 124
  Civil Rights Act (1875)
    banning, 73–74
  Civil Rights Cases of 1883
    reviewed by Supreme
    Court, 74–75, 95
  declared constitutional in
    Plessy v. Ferguson
    segregation decision,
    124
  Fourteenth Amendment
    (1886) prohibition of laws
    protecting, 38, 74
  Katzenbach v. McClung
    (1964) decision on, 73
  treated as a component of
    commerce, 72–76
  See also African Americans
Randolph, Edmund, 63
Rediker, Marcus, 51, 150
Regulations. *See* Government
  regulations; Government
  regulatory agencies
Rent subsidies, 157
Report on Public Credit
  (Hamilton), 152

Retail chains, 5
Revolution. *See* American
  Revolution
Rhode Island's Dorr War
  (1841–1842), 49–51
Richardson, Judge, 94
"Right to Directly Enforce
  People's Rights"
  (Lafayette, Colorado),
  147–148
"Right to survive" amendment
  ballot (Denver, Colorado),
  8–9
Rights. *See* Civil rights;
  Property rights;
  Unalienable rights
Robertson, Mic, 136
Roosevelt, Franklin D., 89
Rotunda, Ronald D., 166
Rousseau, Jean-Jacques,
  32–33
Royal Proclamation of 1763
  (Great Britain), 58–59
Rush, Benjamin, 47

S
Sanborn, Michelle, 187
Sanctuary cities, immigrants'
  rights, 5
*Santa Clara County v. Southern
  Pacific Railroad Company*
  decision, 122–124,
  131–132, 188
Schiesl, Martin, 144–145
Schmader, Stacey, 176

School privatization, 5

Schuyler, Robert L., 60

Segal, Ronald, 54

Segregation
Brown v. Board of Education of Topeka decision prohibiting, 124
declared constitutional in *Plessy v. Ferguson* decision, 124

Self-government right
the American Revolution driven by vision of local, 114–118
Benjamin Franklin's jackass anecdote on, 48, 50
ceiling preemption infringement on, 11–12, 14, 101–102
commerce clause infringing on, 49, 68–73, 82–83
conservative campaign issues that threaten, 145–146
contract clause as tool for taking away community, 89–97
Dorr War (1841–1842) fought over property requirement for, 49–51
global campaign over privilege property rights and, 169–170
government regulations used to deny, 78–79

historic decline of municipal corporations,' 106–109
international trade agreements preempting local legislation and, 118
Plymouth, New Hampshire declaration (2018) example of, 146–147
See also Democracy; Democratic rights

Should Trees Have Standing? (Stone), 42

Shultz, Stanley K., 112

Slaves
Caribbean colonies' law defining property status of, 54
Constitutional three-fifths clause making them privileged property, 16–17, 82–83, 125, 126
Thirteenth Amendment prohibition of involuntary servitude or, 34–36, 75, 84–85, 125
transported to British colonies for labor, 54
widespread distribution in American colonies, 126
See also African Americans; Debt slavery; Property

Smith, Adam, 121, 157–158

Smith, J. Allen, 66, 78–79, 138–140

Social Security privatization
proposal, 172
Sons of Liberty, 127
South African Constitution,
167–168, 169
Southern Pacific Railroad
Company. *See Santa Clara
County v. Southern Pacific
Railroad Company*
decision
Southern Pacific Railroad
Company–Santa Clara
County tax dispute case,
122–124, 131–132
Sovereignty
American Revolution giving
it to the people, 50
ceiling preemption
infringing on state and
local, 11–12, 14
of chartered corporation,
133–134
constitutional limitation of
state and local commerce,
68–70
Spain–Portugal property
division (1493), 30–31, 32
"State actors" status, 82, 132
State constitutions
federal preemption of, 8
petition to amend the state
of Ohio, 185–187
system of law created by
Federalists governing, 1
State government

ceiling preemption by the,
11–12, 14
constitutional limitation of
commerce governance by,
68–70
Dillon's Rule on local
subordination by, 11
examples of recent
enactments subordinating
communities by, 110–111
federal preemption of, 11
making it serve the
governed, 12–15
serving the corporate class,
10–12
See also Government
State regulations
commerce across state
borders free of, 49
as substitute for local
self-governance, 78–79
Stone, Christopher, 42, 43
Story, Joseph, 90–91, 92, 93, 94,
99, 105, 108, 111
Strip mining, 6
Student debt (2018), 160–161
Supreme Court. *See* US
Supreme Court

T
Tamaqua (Schuylkill county,
Pennsylvania)
ordinance protecting
ecosystems passed in,
41–44, 45

"reclamation" plan to fill strip mines with industrial waste in, 41–42

Taxes
Constitutional tax-free zone for trade and wealth creation, 164–165
"creeping socialism" propaganda to promote cutting, 172
"death tax" (inheritance tax), 57
Santa Clara County v. Southern Pacific Railroad Company decision on, 122–124, 131–132, 188
Whiskey Rebellion (1991) over Hamilton's proposed, 153–154, 171

Taylor, John, 155
"The terrors" (England), 150
Texas
House Bill 2595 prohibiting local restrictions on economic property development, 110–111
state legislation banning local fracking bans, 110

Thirteenth Amendment (US Constitution), 34–35, 75, 84–85, 125
Three-fifths clause (US Constitution), 16–17, 82–83, 125, 126
Time magazine, 168

Township Act of 1798 (New Jersey), 104
"Township of the second class" (Pennsylvania), 97–102
Toxic trespass (private poisoning of the public)
Daniel Pennock's death due to exposure to, 178
Fort Gratiot Sanitary Landfill, Inc. v. Michigan Department of National Resources on, 71
Grant Township–PGE dispute over, 97–102
local community groups working to stop, 13–15
Plymouth, New Hampshire declaration (2018) protesting, 146–147
privileged interests blocking control of, 6
Tamaqua ordinance protecting ecosystems from, 41–44
Waste Management Holdings, Inc. decision creating dormant commerce clause permitting, 70–72
See also Environment; Pollution

Trachtenberg, Alan, 140, 141
Trump, Donald, 157
Tyler, John, 50

U

UCLA School of Law, 38

UN *Guiding Principles on Business and Human Rights* (2011), 169–170

Unalienable rights
accumulation of property as not being an, 29, 33–34
Declaration of Independence on self-evident, 3, 21–22, 62–63
"Lancaster Against Pipelines" dispute over justice and interacting, 26–30
New Zealand's recognition of Wanganui River's, 45
Tamaqua ordinance protecting ecosystems and their, 41–44, 45
to withdraw presumed privileges of property when needed, 45–46
See also Citizens; Civil rights
Unequal legal protection blocking solutions to community problems, 5–6
Dillon's Rule promoting, 11, 14, 103–109, 111, 113–114
of personal vs. privileged property, 37–39
See also Corporate personhood

Unequal Protection: How Corporations Became "People"—And How You Can Fight Back (Hartmann), 129

United States
"creeping socialism" propaganda in politics of, 172
European immigration to the, 142–143
history of diminishing returns on democracy for the, 142–145
national debt (2018) of the, 172
"special relationship" between England and, 164
Whiskey Rebellion (1991) in the, 153–154, 171
See also American Revolution

University of Connecticut School of Law, 91

University of Virginia, 168

University of Michigan, 112

Unsustainable energy policies, 6

Urban sewage sludge, 6

US Congress
allowed to declare war by the Constitution, 134
Hamilton's plan to pay Revolution debt proposed to, 152–153

House of Representations of the, 83, 135, 184

Report on Public Credit (Hamilton) sent to, 152

Senate of the, 121

US Constitution

Articles of Confederation replaced by the, 2, 2–3, 59, 60, 61, 69

commerce clause of the, 49, 68–70, 82–83

contract clause in the, 85–86, 88, 154–155

dictatorship of property protected by judicial interpretation of, 4–10

economic self-interest motivating Federalists authors of, 2–4

emulated by newly emancipated nation-states, 20

establishing tax-free zone for trade and wealth creation, 164–165

how democratic rights have been hijacked by the Supreme Court and, 1–4, 16–18

making public law private property, 61–63

oppressive inequalities culture preserved in the, 19–20

ratified in 1789 by Federalists without a Bill of Rights, 160

seen as a charter, 128–129

South African Constitution compared to, 167–168, 169

studies on the declining influence of, 168–170

three-fifths clause of the, 16–17, 82–83, 125, 126

See also Bill of Rights

US Constitution amendments

First Amendment, 87, 125, 133, 181

Fourth Amendment, 132

Fifth Amendment, 87

Thirteenth Amendment, 34–35, 75, 84–85, 125

Fourteenth Amendment, 38, 74, 122, 123, 124, 126, 131

Fifteenth Amendment, 140

Nineteenth Amendment, 140, 145

US Senate, 121

US Supreme Court

Civil Rights Cases of 1883 reviewed by, 74–75, 95

declaring corporate property to be "persons," 2, 18, 38, 75, 79–80, 121–126

dictatorship of property protected by interpretation of, 4–10, 17–18

US Supreme Court (*continued*)
  Dillon's Rule made law of the
    land by the, 103–108, 140
  distinction between public
    and private corporations,
    90
  how democratic rights have
    been hijacked by the, 1–4,
    16–18
  how wealth provides access
    to protection of the, 38–39
  laying groundwork for
    privatizing local
    government, 90–94
  Midnight Judges Act
    reducing number of
    members of, 90
  "private actors" vs. "state
    actors" distinction of, 76,
    82, 132
  retooling the contract clause
    in 1819, 88
  See also Federal judiciary
US Supreme Court decisions
  *Brown v. Board of Education
    of Topeka,* 124
  *Citizens United v. Federal
    Elections Commission*
    (2010), 17–18, 19, 122, 124,
    188
  Dartmouth case, 92–97
  *Fort Gratiot Sanitary
    Landfill, Inc. v. Michigan
    Department of National
    Resources,* 71

Hobby Lobby, 122, 188
Investor State Dispute
  Settlement (ISDS)
  provisions superseding,
  166
Katzenbach v. McClung, 73
Plessy v. Ferguson, 124
*Santa Clara County v.
  Southern Pacific Railroad
  Company* (1886), 122–124,
  131, 188
timeline of establishment of
  corporate personhood
  through, 129–132
*Waste Management
  Holdings, Inc.,* 70–72

V
Versteeg, Mila, 168, 169
Virginia House of Burgesses'
  land grants, 58
Virginia Plan (James Madison),
  62, 66
Voting rights
  Fifteenth Amendment
    giving black males,
    140
  Nineteenth Amendment
    giving women, 140
Voting Rights Act (1965), 75

W
Wages
  Thirteenth Amendment
    prohibition of involuntary

servitude instead of,
34–36, 75, 84–85, 125
"voluntarily" waiving rights
to fair compensation of,
35–37
Waite, Morrison R., 123, 131, 132
Wanganui River (New
Zealand), 45
War debt
British practice of
promissory notes to pay
for, 153
Hamilton's plan to pay
Revolutionary, 152–153
Wartime "privateers," 134
Washington, George, 58–59, 63
Washington University, 168
*Waste Management Holdings,
Inc., et al. v. Gilmore,*
70–71
Water resources
British history of enclosure
or privatization of, 51–55,
150
Nottingham Water Rights
and Local Self-
Government Ordinance
protection of, 52–53
problem of privatization of, 5
See also Environment;
Nature
*We the Corporations: How
American Businesses Won
Their Civil Rights*
(Winkler), 38, 129

Wealth accumulation
American Civil War as
watershed moment in,
121–122
claim to ownership of debtor's
future labor for, 85, 151
commerce clause protection
of, 49, 68–73, 82–83
Constitutional tax-free zone
for trade and, 164–165
Dartmouth case decision
victory for, 92–97, 102,
105, 108, 111, 122–123,
138–139, 188
Federalists' intent to protect,
1–4, 16–18, 19, 29–30,
64–65, 66, 116
how international trade
agreements contribute to,
165–167
how it legitimizes
aristocracy, 67
"Lancaster Against
Pipelines" eminent
domain dispute in context
of, 23–26
opposition to "death tax"
(inheritance tax) of, 57
other people's labor turned
into, 84–85
providing access to
protection of Supreme
Court, 38–39
usury (high interest rates)
creating, 151

Wealth of Nations (Smith), 157–158
Wealthy. *See* Propertied class
Weaver, James B., 135
Webster, Daniel, 94
What Is Property? (Proudhon), 7
Whiskey Rebellion (1991), 153–154, 171
Wile, Rob, 126
Winkler, Adam, 38, 39, 129
Winona County mining ban (Minnesota), 79–80

Wolff, Edward N., 126
Workers' rights, 5
World Trade Organization (WTO), 68, 165–166

Y
Yale University, 140
Yates, Robert, 3
York Daily Record (Pennsylvania), 24

Z
Zinn, Howard, 178

About the Author

Ben is national organizing director for the Community Environmental Legal Defense Fund (CELDF). A lifetime of observation and curiosity about the way people seem to fall into rigid so-  cial categories in industrialized countries eventually led Ben to write this book. He noticed the inflexibility of social class lines from the downside looking up. Curiosity about the source and perpetuation of that unjust arrangement moved him to inquire into how beliefs can overwhelm self-trust in the evidence of our own eyes and ears. That eventually led him to study the way history reflects the past through perceptions biased by class identity.

Ben learned that, hidden deep in the loam of the past, constantly evolving techniques of deception have served the agenda of power and contradict the legends of the founding of civilizations. He learned that privileges for some and servitude for the many constitute an arrangement that has supported the building and maintaining of empire, and that this arrangement is opposed to democracy and justice.

In 2004, Ben joined CELDF and since then has advised and organized in hundreds of communities, many of which adopted CELDF-drafted local laws that codify the rights of human communities and the rights of nature, while advancing social justice and prohibiting activities that violate those rights.

In 2006, Ben worked closely with community leaders and elected officials in Tamaqua, Pennsylvania, in a campaign that resulted in the borough becoming the first community on earth to enact legally enforceable rights for nature. Because of that groundbreaking work, CELDF was invited to Ecuador in 2008 and asked to draft language for the country's Constituent Assembly that would enshrine the rights of Mother Earth. Ecuador's new national constitution was adopted with overwhelming public support, and Ecuador is the first nation on earth to recognize legally enforceable rights for nature.

Ben continues to strive for real local self-government and the rights of nature through his work with colleagues, communities, and the community rights movement.

Berrett–Koehler
Publishers

Berrett-Koehler is an independent publisher dedicated to an ambitious mission: *Connecting people and ideas to create a world that works for all.*

Our publications span many formats, including print, digital, audio, and video. We also offer online resources, training, and gatherings. And we will continue expanding our products and services to advance our mission.

We believe that the solutions to the world's problems will come from all of us, working at all levels: in our society, in our organizations, and in our own lives. Our publications and resources offer pathways to creating a more just, equitable, and sustainable society. They help people make their organizations more humane, democratic, diverse, and effective (and we don't think there's any contradiction there). And they guide people in creating positive change in their own lives and aligning their personal practices with their aspirations for a better world.

And we strive to practice what we preach through what we call "The BK Way." At the core of this approach is *stewardship,* a deep sense of responsibility to administer the company for the benefit of all of our stakeholder groups, including authors, customers, employees, investors, service providers, sales partners, and the communities and environment around us. Everything we do is built around stewardship and our other core values of *quality, partnership, inclusion,* and *sustainability.*

This is why Berrett-Koehler is the first book publishing company to be both a B Corporation (a rigorous certification) and a benefit corporation (a for-profit legal status), which together require us to adhere to the highest standards for corporate, social, and environmental performance. And it is why we have instituted many pioneering practices (which you can learn about at www.bkconnection.com), including the Berrett-Koehler Constitution, the Bill of Rights and Responsibilities for BK Authors, and our unique Author Days.

We are grateful to our readers, authors, and other friends who are supporting our mission. We ask you to share with us examples of how BK publications and resources are making a difference in your lives, organizations, and communities at www.bkconnection.com/impact.

Dear reader,

Thank you for picking up this book and welcome to the worldwide BK community! You're joining a special group of people who have come together to create positive change in their lives, organizations, and communities.

What's BK all about?

Our mission is to connect people and ideas to create a world that works for all.

Why? Our communities, organizations, and lives get bogged down by old paradigms of self-interest, exclusion, hierarchy, and privilege. But we believe that can change. That's why we seek the leading experts on these challenges—and share their actionable ideas with you.

A welcome gift

To help you get started, we'd like to offer you a **free copy** of one of our bestselling ebooks:

www.bkconnection.com/welcome

When you claim your **free ebook**, you'll also be subscribed to our blog.

Our freshest insights

Access the best new tools and ideas for leaders at all levels on our blog at ideas.bkconnection.com.

Sincerely,

Your friends at Berrett-Koehler